More Praise for the Second Edition of *Managing the Unexpected*

"If you are concerned about how your organization will respond to an unexpected event that can easily destroy the reputation and financial health of your organization as well as you as a leader, this is the book for you. You will learn from two world-renowned experts what makes organizations susceptible to unexpected catastrophic events and what you can do to make your organization alert and responsive to unexpected and potentially destructive events."

—**Michael Beer,** professor emeritus, Harvard Business School
    and chairman, TruePoint Partners

"Improving patient safety has, at long last, risen high on the priority list—where it belongs—for health care leaders. But, as those leaders soon realize, protecting and improving safety and reliability in complex systems is not easy. Simple formulae won't work. Luckily, the technical and social sciences that underlie safe practice have been developing for many decades in sectors other than health care, with the scholarship and teaching of experts like Weick and Sutcliffe. *Managing the Unexpected* is a *tour de force*, as it explains and illustrates much of what is now known about organizational and social systems that can achieve high reliability. I know of no better introduction to safety at the state-of-the-art, and it is the first book I now recommend to health care leaders who ask me how they can best deepen their knowledge of this fascinating and crucially important field. Adapting its lessons to the world of patient care is not just possible; if we are to achieve our mission in health care, it is essential."

—**Donald M. Berwick,** MD, MPP, president and CEO,
    Institute for Healthcare Improvement

"What can a manager in a global firm learn from local forest firefighters in California? Plenty. As businesses fragment their value chains and depend on a wide variety of global suppliers, their systems become fragile. There are more moving parts, few of which they directly own or control. The interlinkages are also continuously changing. In *Managing the Unexpected*, Weick and Sutcliffe provide an extraordinary blueprint for creating high reliability organizations in which the unexpected is the norm. Capacity to create new knowledge rapidly, substituting collaborative and integrative capacity for investment capacity, and seeing new patterns in weak signals are critical to building a culture that the authors call 'mindfulness' in managing. The insights in this book are a must for those who want to remain at the cutting edge."

—**C. K. Prahalad,** The Paul and Ruth McCracken
    Distinguished University Professor of Corporate Strategy,
    The Ross School of Business, University of Michigan

"For me, Karl Weick and Kathleen Sutcliffe are the giants of the risk and resilience business. Their writings have consistently excited, inspired, and informed me over many years now. They are always beautifully written, always innovative, and marvelously rich in stories and wise paradoxes. They are a joy to read.

"I am not surprised that the first edition of *Managing the Unexpected* has proved to be such a big hit. It reaches out equally to managers and to fellow social scientists. The book translates the five defining characteristics of high reliability organizations (HROs) into a comprehensive program for dealing mindfully with unforeseen, unanticipated, and often unwanted happenings in a variety of risky domains.

"The second edition goes still further. Prominent among its new features is a brilliant chapter that describes a change program built around small shifts and alterations that produce visible and tangible results. This 'small wins strategy' is again organized around the five defining principles of HROs: preoccupation with failure, resistance to simplification, sensitivity to the details of operations, commitment to resilience, and deference to expertise. Firefighting, both in its organized form and in its day-to-day reality, is a central theme of this chapter. I found it enriching and full of surprises. This book about dealing with the unexpected is rightly full of unexpected challenges to conventional managerial wisdom. It is perhaps the best thing they have written. I can give it no higher praise. Buy it and live by it."

—**James Reason,** author, *Managing the Risks of Organizational Accidents*

"The quality of responses by organizational leaders at every level to unexpected events and developments either strengthen or weaken the system. The unexpected can, therefore, be a turning point in the fortunes of organizations and their leaders. Do the right things—like J&J's leaders in the Tylenol crisis—and your stock (metaphorically and literally) will rise. Do the wrong things—like the leaders of FEMA post-Katrina—and you will lose respect and more. But leaders can't wait until the crisis hits—they have to prepare their organizations and keep them tuned. Weick and Sutcliffe offer valuable insights and practical advice to improve the odds that you will be leading a high reliability organization when the chips are down."

—**B. Joseph White,** president, University of Illinois

Managing the Unexpected

Karl E. Weick
Kathleen M. Sutcliffe

JB JOSSEY-BASS

Managing the Unexpected

Resilient Performance in an Age of Uncertainty

Second Edition

John Wiley & Sons, Inc.

Published by Jossey-Bass
A Wiley Imprint
989 Market Street, San Francisco, CA 94103-1741   www.josseybass.com

Wiley Bicentennial logo: Richard J. Pacifico

Readers should be aware that Internet Web sites offered as citations and/or sources for further information may have changed or disappeared between the time this was written and when it is read.

Limit of Liability/Disclaimer of Warranty: While the publisher and author have used their best efforts in preparing this book, they make no representations or warranties with respect to the accuracy or completeness of the contents of this book and specifically disclaim any implied warranties of merchantability or fitness for a particular purpose. No warranty may be created or extended by sales representatives or written sales materials. The advice and strategies contained herein may not be suitable for your situation. You should consult with a professional where appropriate. Neither the publisher nor author shall be liable for any loss of profit or any other commercial damages, including but not limited to special, incidental, consequential, or other damages.

Jossey-Bass books and products are available through most bookstores. To contact Jossey-Bass directly call our Customer Care Department within the U.S. at 800-956-7739, outside the U.S. at 317-572-3986, or fax 317-572-4002.

Jossey-Bass also publishes its books in a variety of electronic formats. Some content that appears in print may not be available in electronic books.

Library of Congress Cataloging-in-Publication Data
Weick, Karl E.
  Managing the unexpected : resilient performance in an age
of uncertainty / Karl E. Weick, Kathleen M. Sutcliffe. —2nd ed.
    p. cm.
  Includes bibliographical references and index.
  ISBN 978-0-7879-9649-9 (cloth)
1. Crisis management. 2. Leadership. 3. Industrial management.
I. Sutcliffe, Kathleen M., 1950- II. Title.
  HD49.W45 2007
  658.4'056—dc22

                                                  2007024496

Printed in the United States of America
SECOND EDITION
HB Printing   10 9 8 7 6

Contents

Preface

With the unexpected becoming a larger chunk of everyday life, it isn't surprising that we find ourselves interested in resilience and coping. Since the publication of the first edition of *Managing the Unexpected*, the unexpected has surfaced time and time again. Hurricane Katrina, the Asian tsunami, the Enron scandal, the *Columbia* space shuttle disaster, terrorist attacks such as 9/11, the London bombings, and the Madrid train disaster, all on a large scale, have tested the stability of our organizations. Most organizations experience unexpected events on a much smaller scale all the time. These dynamic and uncertain times raise the questions of how and why some organizations are much more capable than others of maintaining function and structure in the face of drastic change and of bouncing back in a stronger position to tackle future challenges.

A Book About Reliable Organizations

This book is based on examination of the ways people and organizations organize for high performance in settings where the potential for error and disaster is overwhelming: nuclear aircraft carriers, air traffic control systems, aircraft operations systems, hostage negotiation teams, emergency medical treatment teams, nuclear power generation plants, continuous processing firms, and wildland firefighting crews. These diverse organizations share a singular demand: They have no choice but to function reliably. If reliability is compromised, severe harm results. Adopting the terminology first used by researchers at the University of California, Berkeley, we have lumped these organizations together and called them high reliability organizations (HROs).

Other people who have examined these organizations were struck by their unique structural features. We saw something else. These organizations also think and act differently. Their processes and practices are different, but not in ways that are uniquely different.

Like most other business organizations, HROs experience unexpected problems continually, and most of those problems involve a lapse in reliability. Either somebody counts on something to happen and it doesn't, or someone counts on something not to happen and it does. And most of these lapses do not emerge abruptly as full-blown issues. Instead, small clues accumulate for some time and suggest that unexpected things are happening and aren't going away.

Benchmarking Against the Experts

Given today's dynamic and uncertain business environments, it is important to benchmark on the experts in managing the unexpected. This book is about experts in resilient high performance and how they stay on top of operations, despite repeated interruptions. Part of their success stems from their uncommon skill at finding ways to stay mindful about what is happening. They update their ideas of current situations and are not held captive by old categories or crude renderings of the contexts they face. They use techniques that you can copy—techniques that are worth copying because they ensure faster learning, more alert sensing, and better relationships with customers. Unreliable suppliers and unreliable services make us crazy. But much to our surprise, reliability does not mean a complete lack of variation. It's just the opposite. It takes mindful variety to ensure stable high performance. HROs have learned that the hard way. We hope to make it easier for you to learn the same lessons they learned the hard way.

When we say that these are lessons learned the hard way, we mean that these principles come out of HRO experiences with success and failure. And frequently, the principles are more visible in experiences of failure, which is why several examples in this book focus on mismanagement of the unexpected. What we find striking about HROs is that they have dealt with these issues for a long time and know what they understand and what they don't understand. When we ask you to benchmark on these organizations, we do so not because they "have it right" but because they struggle to get it right on a continuing basis. Complacency and hubris are two of their biggest enemies. Once you study their experiences, we hope they will be your enemies as well.

Acknowledgments

Several people figured in this project, and we want to express our appreciation for their help. We are especially grateful to a host of valued colleagues whose work we admire, people such as Bob Bea, Gary Klein, Constance Perin, Charles Perrow, Paul Schulman, Scott Snook, Bill Starbuck, Diane Vaughan, David Woods, and especially "the mother of HROs," Karlene Roberts.

We have learned a great deal about managing the unexpected from members of the wildland firefighting community, including Anne Black, Paul Chamberlin, Dave Christianson, Jim Cooke, Mike DeGrosky, Deirdre Dether, Riva Duncan, Brett Fay, Paul Keller, Mark Linane, Paul Linse, Paula Nasiatka, Ted Putnam, Jim Saveland, and Dave Thomas. Marlys Christianson, Marilynn Rosenthal, Daved van Stralen, and Bob Wears have helped us understand adverse events in medical settings. We also thank Michelle Barton, Dan Gruber, and all our colleagues at the Ross School of Business at the University of Michigan. David Obstfeld played an important role in helping us synthesize early ideas. Kathleen Sutcliffe continues to learn from people who have no choice but to show up and manage it all, including Carolen Hope, Steve Lyford, Gail Marnik, Fiona and Miranda Marnik-Said, John Said, and Frances Sanders.

Finally, we dedicate this book to the two people who always clear space and time for us to be able to do our best work. Karen

Weick is a beloved expert at managing the unexpected, and half of this book is directly traceable to her efforts. The other half of the book is traceable to Tim Wintermute, who for Kathleen makes it all worthwhile. We dedicate this book to both of them with love!

June 2007   Karl E. Weick
Ann Arbor, Michigan   Kathleen M. Sutcliffe

Managing the Unexpected

1

Managing the Unexpected

What Business Can Learn from High Reliability Organizations

Unexpected events often audit our resilience. They affect how much we stretch without breaking and then how well we recover. Some of those audits are mild. But others are brutal. This book is about both kinds of audits, as unrecognized mild audits often turn brutal.

Consider some examples. People did not expect that Pentium computer chips would make incorrect calculations, that a new soft drink formula would unleash protests rather than praise, that bottled water would be tainted with benzene, that fresh spinach would cause serious illness, that pet food would be tainted with poison, that patients supposedly suffering from St. Louis encephalitis were actually victims of the West Nile virus, or that pediatric deaths during cardiac surgery would be excessive. All of these were the mild audits that grew into substantial problems for Intel, Coca-Cola, Perrier, Salinas Valley spinach growers, Menu Foods, the Centers for Disease Control and Prevention, and the Bristol Royal Infirmary, respectively. In each case, small failures went unnoticed, simple diagnoses were accepted, frontline operations were taken for granted, recovery was treated as routine, and experts deferred to authorities. These troubled organizations might have acted differently had they modeled themselves after a family of organizations that operate continuously under trying conditions and have fewer than their fair share of major incidents. These *high reliability organizations* (HROs) practice a form of organizing that reduces the brutality of audits and speeds up the process of recovering. They are the focus of this book.

The Basic Message of This Book

This book is about organizations, expectations, and mindfulness. Our basic message is that expectations can get you into trouble unless you create a mindful infrastructure that continually does all of the following:

- Tracks small failures
- Resists oversimplification
- Remains sensitive to operations
- Maintains capabilities for resilience
- Takes advantage of shifting locations of expertise

Failure to move toward this type of mindful infrastructure magnifies the damage produced by unexpected events and impairs reliable performance. Moving toward a mindful infrastructure is harder than it looks because it means that people have to forgo the "pleasures" of attending to success, simplicities, strategy, planning, and superiors.

This first chapter presents an overview of what it takes to organize for high reliability. We anchor this overview in a devastating incident, the Cerro Grande wildland fire, which caused $1 billion of damage to Los Alamos, New Mexico, and the adjacent Los Alamos National Laboratories in May 2000. As you will see, events overwhelmed a crew and a system that planned to burn out a hazardous 300-acre area at the Bandelier National Monument. Without much warning, unexpected winds forced the system to deal with a task that was exactly the opposite of the one they were prepared for. Instead of managing an intentional prescribed burn, people in the system suddenly had to suppress an unintentional active fire that had escaped its intended boundaries. Although the Cerro Grande fire is a dramatic event, it involves moments of organizing that are common to organizations of all kinds. The organizing for the Cerro Grande fire started with a plan, vague notions of contingency resources, incomplete knowledge of the system, unexpected changes in staffing, uneven communication, quotas, and shifting command structures. When the unexpected wind swirled into this system, the vagueness, the incompleteness, and the shifting command were the weak points that gave way.

The Cerro Grande Fire: A Brutal Audit

Consider Pat Lagadec's vivid words: "The ability to deal with a crisis situation is largely dependent on the structures that have been developed before chaos arrives. The event can in some ways be considered as an abrupt and brutal audit: at a moment's notice, everything that was left unprepared becomes a complex problem, and every weakness comes rushing to the forefront."[1]

Lagadec's description pinpoints potential threats to managing the unexpected. "Structures developed before the crisis arrives" include both routines and special resources for the crisis such as SWAT teams. All of these help people deal with the disruption, except that the crises that are envisioned seldom resemble the crises that actually unfold. This mismatch means that a brutal audit uncovers vulnerability in the form of unforeseen collapses in functioning.

A brutal audit also uncovers unforeseen weakness in resilience— the capability to recover. Resilient action that enables recovery from setbacks is built out of a broad repertoire of action and experience, the ability to recombine fragments of past experience into novel responses, emotional control, skill at respectful interaction,[2] and knowledge of how the system functions. Structures of resilience reflect lessons that HROs have learned the hard way. The best HROs know that they have not experienced all of the ways that their system can fail. They also know that they have not deduced all possible failure modes. And they have a deep appreciation for the liabilities of overconfidence. This appreciation takes the form of ongoing mindfulness embedded in practices that enact alertness, broaden attention, reduce distractions, and forestall misleading simplifications. How HROs pull this off, and how you can do the same, are what this book is about. For the moment, the key point is that ongoing mindful practice reduces the severity and frequency of brutal audits, accelerates recovery, and facilitates learning from the audit.

The Events at Cerro Grande

The successes as well as the failures of wildland firefighters can teach us a lot about managing the unexpected.

Normally, wildland firefighting is reactive, as is true for most settings where people describe themselves figuratively as "putting out fires." Reactive action occurs when firefighters respond to fires that are already burning (such as those started by lightning). Reactive action among nonfirefighters occurs when they respond to "fires" lit by disgruntled customers, shifts in financial markets, or supply chain breakdowns. Wildland firefighting, however, has become more *proactive* and preemptive as forests have become more dangerous due to dead trees and debris on the forest floor. When fires break out in debris-laden forests, they burn faster and hotter, are more difficult to control, and can threaten a larger number of homes and businesses. To prevent such disasters, crews now ignite small preemptive fires, which they try to contain within prescribed areas. A prescribed burn reduces the fuel load that could lead to much larger fires. But prescribed fires are complex events. "Because of the potential for unintended consequences, prescribed fire is one of the highest-risk activities land management agencies undertake. Contingency planning, which includes identifying necessary resources should a planned ignition exceed prescription parameters, is an essential component of a burn plan."[3]

The prescribed burn at Cerro Grande was just such a preemptive, prescribed fire. Plans were made to burn 300 acres in the upper portion of the 32,727-acre Bandelier National Monument near Santa Fe, New Mexico (see Figure 1.1). The area of the burn was a south-facing slope between 9,000 and 10,000 feet elevation with a 2 to 20 percent rise.

Figure 1.1 Bandelier National Monument and Vicinity

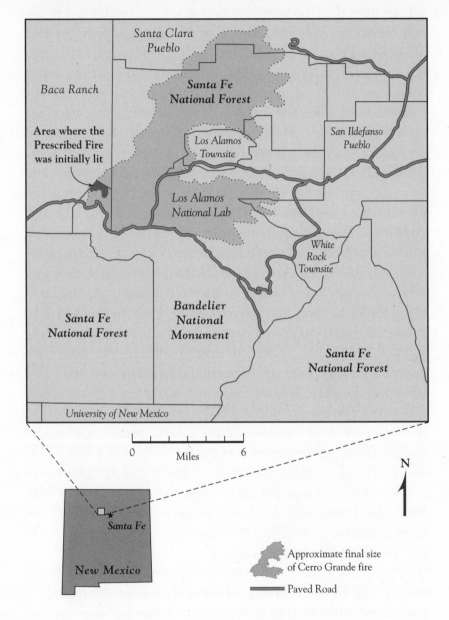

Santa Clara Pueblo

Baca Ranch

Santa Fe National Forest

Area where the Prescribed Fire was initially lit

Los Alamos Townsite

San Ildefanso Pueblo

Los Alamos National Lab

White Rock Townsite

Santa Fe National Forest

Bandelier National Monument

Santa Fe National Forest

University of New Mexico

0   Miles   6

N

Santa Fe

New Mexico

Approximate final size of Cerro Grande fire

Paved Road

Thursday evening, May 4, 2000, a crew of ten Black Mesa fire-fighters from the Northern Pueblo Agency and ten United States Park Service firefighters plus a fire observer (renowned firefighter Paul Gleason) made a 1-acre test burn at 7:20 P.M. to see whether the grass was dry enough to continue with the planned burn. The test was successful, and at 8:00 P.M., the ignition crew began to insert fire into the prescribed area. Their first action was to create a blackline around the outside edge of the planned burn area, starting on the east side. To construct a blackline, a drip torch is used to ignite the grass, the fire is allowed to burn a path about 3 feet wide, and then the outer and inner edges of the fire are extinguished. A blackline prevents unintended fire spread later when the actual prescribed burn is ignited. As the ignition proceeded, the inner edge of the blackline proved hard to extinguish, so the burn boss,[4] Mike Powell, decided to extinguish only the outer edge and to let the inner edge keep burning into an area that was to be burned out later in the season. Around midnight, the Black Mesa crew was responding slowly and seemed to be exhausted. Burn boss Powell, fearing that the crew members might endanger themselves because of their condition, sent them back down the mountain along with five of the Park Service people. This left only six people to hold the surprisingly active fire, two on the west side and four on the east side. At 3:00 Friday morning, Powell called the dispatcher at the regional Santa Fe Zone Dispatch center and requested a fresh crew of twenty hotshots for 7:00 that morning. To his surprise, Powell heard the dispatcher say that he couldn't approve this and would have to wait and ask his supervisor who came in at 7:00. In disbelief, Powell tried to call other people he knew to help him and finally contacted a two-person Bandelier National Monument fire engine crew who did arrive at 6:00 A.M.

Paul Gleason had been observing the firing operation earlier in the evening. He was to be the burn boss of a fire in the same area at a later date and wanted to survey the site. When Gleason returned to the fire at 6:00 Friday morning, he was worried about two things: the fire was moving faster than expected, and no fresh resources had been ordered. Powell again tried to call Santa Fe dispatch, but this time no one answered the phone. Gleason then called the Bande-lier Monument superintendent, Roy Weaver, and explained the problem. After heated negotiations between dispatch (which began to answer the phone again at 7:30 A.M.) and Bandelier personnel over who would pay for the requested resources, Gleason got a promise that a twenty-person crew would be there at 9:00 A.M. and that a helicopter would be there shortly thereafter to drop water on the flames. Gleason took over the burn boss duties at 10:00 A.M. and told Powell to get some sleep. The crew that was promised for 9:00 did not arrive until 11:00, and the helicopter arrived at 10:30 without a water bucket. Partly because insufficient resources were focused on the fire, it spotted and "slopped over" the fireline on the east side, igniting combustible bunchgrass. At 1:00 P.M. Friday, the fire escaped the prescribed burn area and was declared a wildland fire that now had to be extinguished. The suppression strategy was to adopt an indirect attack, which meant that backfires would be lit some distance away from the current flames. These backfires, however, were lit in an area that was scheduled to be burned later in the spring. The intent of the backfiring was to remove fuel that would accelerate the escaping fire.

This plan worked well from Friday until Sunday at 11:50 A.M. when unexpected winds of up to 50 miles per hour blew in from the west and shoved the fire into adjacent canyons. These canyons channeled the winds and intensified their speed, both of which effects increased the flame heights and the rapidity with which the fire moved. The fire exploded toward the city and laboratories of Los Alamos, eighteen thousand people were evacuated, and by late Tuesday, 235 homes had burned to the ground and thirty-nine laboratory buildings had been destroyed. The fire, started on May 4, was finally stopped on May 19 after it had been fought by one thousand firefighters, consumed 48,000 acres, and inflicted $1 billion worth of damage. As Ed Hiatt, one of the firefighters on the east side, reported, "It all started with a one-inch-wide band of fire that crept across the fireline into fresh grass." This tiny spot fire kept flaring up every time firefighters thought they had put it out.

Understanding the Events at Cerro Grande

A one-inch band of fire that produces $1 billion in damage is a classic pattern in unexpected events. Small events have large consequences. Small discrepancies give off small clues that are hard to spot but easy to treat if they are spotted. When clues become much more visible, they are that much harder to treat. Managing the unexpected often means that people have to make strong responses to weak signals, something that is counterintuitive and not very "heroic." Normally, we make weak responses to weak signals and strong responses to strong signals.

To understand more clearly what happened at Cerro Grande, we can compare how the burn project was organized with the ways that HROs are organized. As we said earlier, systems that mismanage the unexpected tend to ignore small failures, accept simple diagnoses, take frontline operations for granted, neglect capabilities for resilience, and defer to authorities rather than experts.[5] Fragments of this pattern are visible in Cerro Grande.

To start, think about what the members of the team at Cerro Grande expected. They expected that their burn plan was doable and met objectives, that the fire itself would be of low to moderate complexity, that they had a capable crew and resources, that the dispatch system was reliable and responsive, that contingency resources were on standby, that weather forecasts did not preclude burning, and that local conditions (such as low residual dampness despite recent snow) were at a preparedness level such that burning was possible. The very fact that so much of the success of this project was tied to these expectations suggests the importance of continuing mindfulness to see if expectations were being fulfilled and to catch early indications that they weren't. One way to be more mindful of emerging unintended consequences is to apply the principles of high reliability organizing. As you will see, early clues that expectations were being frustrated began to pile up and endanger the project.

To continue our analysis, let us reintroduce the five key ideas of mindful infrastructure, viewing each one now as a principle underlying the performance of highly reliable organizations. As we will discuss more fully in later chapters, the first three principles involve mainly an HRO's capacity to anticipate "unexpected" problems, while the fourth and fifth have more to do with capacity to contain them. You will see the extent to which the system that attempted to control the Cerro Grande incident was able to implement these principles.

HRO Principle 1: Preoccupation with Failure. HROs are distinctive because they are *preoccupied with failure*. They treat any lapse as a symptom that something may be wrong with the system, something that could have severe consequences if several separate small errors happened to coincide. For example, the disastrous release of 40 tons of methyl isocyanate gas used by Union Carbide in the manufacture of pesticides killed three thousand people initially on December 3, 1984, in Bhopal, India.[6] Small errors such as the failure to reinsert a water isolation plate, malfunctioning storage tanks, inoperative gauges and alarms, English-language manuals that could not be read by plant personnel, and high turnover with a consequent loss of experience all contributed to the disaster. HROs encourage reporting of errors, they elaborate experiences of a near miss for what can be learned, and they are wary of the potential liabilities of success, including complacency, the temptation to reduce margins of safety, and the drift into automatic processing. They also make a continuing effort to articulate mistakes they don't want to make and assess the likelihood that strategies increase the risk of triggering these mistakes.

At the Cerro Grande fire, there were several small failures that signaled larger problems. For example, agencies that managed land adjacent to Bandelier were nervous about the planned burn because four prescribed fires nearby had escaped their intended boundaries in the two weeks prior to the planned Cerro Grande burn.[7] Furthermore, there were two small but significant failures once the fire was ignited Thursday night. First, the inability to extinguish the inner edge of the blackline burn suggested a more active fire than had been anticipated. Once the fire was allowed to burn freely inside the blackline, the crew lost the option *not* to ignite the interior fire. Second, the release of personnel at midnight reduced the ability of the on-site crew to deal with further unexpected events. Once the Black Mesa crew left the mountain, there was only a skeleton crew left to handle whatever came up. These failures, coupled with temporary staffing of the dispatch center and the dispatcher's refusal to order a fresh twenty-person crew meant that small failures were beginning to pile up.[8] These weak signals of failure required a stronger response that could mobilize fresh resources. While there were growing signals of system failure, each signal was itself weak and was handled with a weak response. The burn boss tried to locate fresh resources by calling people he knew, but he reached only two people who said they would arrive at 6:00 A.M.

HRO Principle 2: Reluctance to Simplify. Another way HROs manage for the unexpected is by being *reluctant to accept simplifications*. It is certainly true that success in any coordinated activity requires that people simplify in order to stay focused on a handful of key issues and key indicators. But it is also true that less simplification allows you to see more. HROs take deliberate steps to create more complete and nuanced pictures of what they face and who they are as they face it. Knowing that the world they face is complex, unstable, unknowable, and unpredictable, HROs position themselves to see as much as possible. They welcome diverse experience, skepticism toward received wisdom, and negotiating tactics that reconcile differences of opinion without destroying the nuances that diverse people detect. When they "recognize" an event as something they have experienced before and understood, that recognition is a source of concern rather than comfort. The concern is that superficial similarities between the present and the past mask deeper differences that could prove fatal.[9] For example, the burst of debris at the root of the left wing of the *Columbia* space shuttle, which was observed 82 seconds into the launch on January 16, 2003, was interpreted as an event that was "almost in-family." By this, NASA top management meant that the event was largely analyzed, reportable, and understood. They were wrong.

Simplification played a necessary but also disrupting role in Cerro Grande as it does in other efforts to organize for reliable functioning. The burn plan was constructed on the basis of ratings of how complex the burn was likely to be. Ratings of complexity convert information about things like elevations (steep slope versus flat land), fuel types (short grass, open timber, long-needle litter under a closed stand of timber), changes in weather, and other local conditions (such as private land adjacent to the burn area) into a number that simplifies those features.

But the complexity of the Cerro Grande burn was misestimated because the wrong system was used to predict how complicated the burn would be. Burn boss Powell rated the complexity of the burn using a scale of 1–2–3 to rate individual contingencies where 3 was high complexity. However, he should have used a National Park Service scale of 1–3–5 where 5 was high complexity.[10] He used the incorrect scale because it was posted on the Internet and no one at the five federal wildland agencies had detected the incorrect posting.[11] The incorrect scale, which Powell used correctly, estimated that the fire would be of low to moderate complexity. Had the correct rating scale been used, the sum of the same individual ratings would have indicated that the fire would be of moderate to high complexity. This difference is important because as a burn boss, Powell was qualified to direct a low complexity event but not a high-complexity event. Furthermore, the number of resources needed to hold the fire to the prescribed area and the number that need to be on standby are greater for high-complexity burns and greater than the number that were requested for Cerro Grande.[12]

There were other troublesome simplifications. Planners misjudged the intensity of individual elements that were summed into the overall complexity rating. This was true for at least one of the three categories of elements—the three being threats to boundaries, fuels and fire behavior, and objectives.[13] Each misjudgment erred in the direction of underestimating difficulty. Finally, all of these ratings were completed weeks before the burn and were not reevaluated on the day of the burn, most probably because such updating is not required by policy.[14]

The members of the burn crew did exhibit some reluctance to simplify when they conducted a test burn. The data from the test burn can be used to update earlier judgments of complexity. We say "can be used" because, as with all projects that are under way, people are prone to interpret new data in ways that confirm their expectations. It is hard to spot signs that burning is unwise when twenty people are standing around ready to start the burn.

There is no question that when you organize, you simplify. But you don't need to simplify casually or habitually or instantly. People can be more deliberate in their choices of what to simplify. To be more deliberate means to be more thorough in articulating mistakes you don't want to make. In the case of prescribed burns, one mistake you don't want to make is to misjudge the complexity of the burn. As the Cerro Grande Board of Inquiry said, there are strong links among complexity ratings, resources deployed and on standby, and contingency plans.[15] If simplifications lead to misspecification of any one of those elements, brutal audits are more likely. Again, this is not a problem unique to the world of firefighting. Everyone makes assumptions about how complex a project will be, what resources are needed to complete the project, and how to avoid entrapment. Those assumptions can be rough or nuanced. Resilience lies in the direction of nuance.

HRO Principle 3: Sensitivity to Operations. HROs are *sensitive to operations*. They are attentive to the front line, where the real work gets done. The "big picture" in HROs is less strategic and more situational than is true of most other organizations. When people have well-developed situational awareness, they can make the continuous adjustments that prevent errors from accumulating and enlarging.[16] Anomalies are noticed while they are still tractable and can still be isolated. All of this is made possible because HROs are aware of the close ties between sensitivity to operations and sensitivity to relationships. People who refuse to speak up out of fear undermine the system, which knows less than it needs to know to work effectively. People in HROs know that you can't develop a big picture of operations if the symptoms of those operations are withheld. It makes no difference whether they are withheld for relational reasons such as fear, ignorance, or indifference. If managers refuse to examine what happens between heads, they'll be eternally puzzled by what appears to happen inside individual heads.

When Santa Fe dispatch finally picked up the phone at 7:30 A.M. Friday morning, a stalemate occurred. The burn boss was finally able to request a fresh twenty-person crew. Dispatch asked, "Are you declaring this an escaped fire?" The swift reply was, "No, I'm trying to prevent it from becoming an escaped fire." To which dispatch replied, "I can't release fresh resources until it is declared an escaped fire." Conflicting interpretations of policy stalled operations until the issues were sorted out. Park Service personnel managing the burn believed that once the availability of contingency resources had been confirmed in the burn plan, they would be available if requested. Dispatch, however, interpreted the policy as saying that contingency resources would be made available only when a prescribed fire escaped and was declared a wildfire.[17]

While all the haggling was going on, the fire kept getting bigger and the exhausted skeleton crew members found it harder and harder to keep the blaze from circling around behind them. As Paul Gleason said after the event, "If someone phones and needs help, don't talk budget. This is fire! Do the money thing later."[18]

Budgets are often insensitive to operations. The problem at Cerro Grande was that budgets were insensitive to operations three times over. First, they were insensitive to the need for instant activation of standby resources to back up the frontline workers. Second, they were insensitive because there were conflicting definitions of "standby resources." Standby was interpreted to mean either available in the area or unassigned to other activities and available for immediate support.[19] Third, the budgeting operations themselves were poorly understood, which meant that the system was insensitive to bottlenecks in its own functioning.

Many readers will see these insensitivities and stalemates as normal and natural trouble whenever interactions occur between agencies, divisions, silos, jurisdictions, or functions. Although insensitivity may be normal trouble, it becomes big trouble when unexpected audits dissolve coordination that was tenuous to begin with.

HRO Principle 4: Commitment to Resilience. No system is perfect. HROs know this as well as anyone. This is why they complement their anticipatory activities of learning from failure, complicating their perceptions, and remaining sensitive to operations with a *commitment to resilience*. "The essence of resilience is therefore the intrinsic ability of an organization (system) to maintain or regain a dynamically stable state, which allows it to continue operations after a major mishap and/or in the presence of a continuous stress."[20] HROs develop capabilities to detect, contain, and bounce back from those inevitable errors that are part of an indeterminate world.[21] The hallmark of an HRO is not that it is error-free but that errors don't disable it.

Resilience is a combination of keeping errors small and of improvising workarounds that allow the system to keep functioning. Both of these pathways to resilience demand deep knowledge of the technology, the system, one's coworkers, and most of all, oneself. HROs put a premium on training, personnel with deep and varied experience, and skills of recombination and making do with whatever is at hand. They imagine worst-case conditions[22] and practice their own equivalent of fire drills. Psychologist Gary Klein, an expert in high-stakes decision making, suggests that the most effective fire commanders have rich fantasy lives and mentally simulate potential lines of attack.[23]

The Cerro Grande fire makes several problems of resilience more visible. The system keeps getting stretched. But it never quite recovers to the point where it started on Thursday or to a point that fosters continued coping. Consider the crew itself. Crew members had reported for work at 7:00 A.M. Thursday morning, May 4, and had been used from that time on to preposition tools and equipment at the top of the hill. This meant that they were walking up a steep slope carrying heavy equipment, a hike that took 90 minutes to reach the top. They did this several times. The burn itself was supposed to be lit in the afternoon but was postponed until evening, which kept the crew on site longer. Recall that the Black Mesa holding crew was released from the fire at midnight, which increased the burden on the workers who stayed behind. Finally, the remaining crew had been working for close to thirty hours by the time fresh resources arrived late Friday morning. The normal work-rest cycle is sixteen hours on, eight hours off (a ratio of 2 to 1).[24] The capabilities for recovery, containment, fresh thinking, and creative solutions to unexpected problems were severely diminished.

Formal investigations conducted in the aftermath of the Cerro Grande fire circled around the question of whether the burn boss was sufficiently "aggressive" in conveying "a sense of urgency" regarding the need for fresh resources.[25] Answers to that question remain in dispute. But what is not in dispute is that the unavailability of fresh resources at 7:00 A.M. Friday morning meant that exhausted firefighters had to cope with the unexpected spot fires and slopover of fire on the east side until relief came late Friday morning. Try as they might, the overextended crew simply could not handle the setbacks the way a fresh crew could. The crew at Cerro Grande was losing its flexibility as well as its ability to restore the lost flexibility. A nondynamic crew was facing a dynamic environment. That spells trouble.

HRO Principle 5: *Deference to Expertise*. The final distinctive feature of HROs is their *deference to expertise*. HROs cultivate diversity, not just because it helps them notice more in complex environments, but also because it helps them do more with the complexities they do spot. Rigid hierarchies have their own special vulnerability to error. Errors at higher levels tend to pick up and combine with errors at lower levels, thereby making the resulting problem bigger, harder to comprehend, and more prone to escalation.

To prevent this deadly scenario, HROs push decision making down and around.[26] Decisions are made on the front line, and authority migrates to the people with the most expertise, regardless of their rank. This is not simply a case of people deferring to the person with the "most experience." Experience by itself is no guarantee of expertise, since all too often people have the same experience over and over and do little to elaborate those repetitions. The pattern of decisions "migrating" to expertise is found in flight operations on aircraft carriers, where "uniqueness coupled with the need for accurate decisions leads to decisions that 'search' for the expert and migrate around the organization. The decisions migrate around these organizations in search of a person who has specific knowledge of the event."[27]

Issues of expertise, authority, and deference were complicated at Cerro Grande, as they are in everyday life. There was deference to the person at Cerro Grande who had the most expertise, Paul Gleason. He is a legend in the fire world. Gleason intervened to solve the impasse over fresh resources, agreed to be burn boss Friday morning so that Mike Powell could get some sleep, assumed the position of incident commander when the fire escaped on Friday at 1:00, and continued as incident commander when the fire exploded on Sunday until a complete incident command team could get to the fire. Gleason received the deference he deserved, but there were two problems. First, he made good decisions, but many were not implemented. Second, he may have been the object of too much deference. This is an easy point to misunderstand. There is the remote possibility that the sheer power of Gleason's expertise led others on the scene to let up in their monitoring of the situation in the belief that if something were amiss, a person of Gleason's stature would surely catch it.[28] In other words, if Gleason doesn't see it, it's not happening. Gleason was well aware of his own limitations and fallibilities. But others may not have been. In their veneration of Gleason, they inadvertently discounted their own impressions of the fire, which could have captured details that Gleason missed.

But there was also too little deference to expertise in the events preceding the blowup at Cerro Grande. Anyone in a dispatcher role is less of an expert on specific fire behavior than the on-scene person who is face to face with the fire. Likewise, a temporary dispatcher is less of an expert on local practices and personnel than the regular dispatcher assigned to a post. A dispatcher who waits to make a decision until his superior arrives at 7:00 A.M. rather than try to fill the urgent needs of an on-scene fire boss at 3:00 A.M. clearly defers to authority rather than to expertise. How aggressively that expertise was asserted at 3:00 A.M. can be debated. But less debatable is where that expertise was located.

Cerro Grande and the Concept of Mindful Management

Is Cerro Grande really that different from what all of us experience? Is it really all that rare to have optimistic plans, insufficient staff, misestimated complexity, broken promises, overlooked details, turf battles, loss of control, unanticipated consequences? No! The board of inquiry said as much when it described judgments at Cerro Grande as "not arbitrary, capricious, or unreasonable in light of the information they had prior to the burn."[29] But the information prior to the burn could have been better. And the information during the burn could have been much better. For example, it is not clear whether the dispatcher knew that the Black Mesa crew had left the mountain when Powell called in at 3:00 A.M. requesting fresh resources.

What does it mean, then, to manage an unexpected event well? Good management of the unexpected is *mindful* management. That answer comes from careful study of high reliability organizations,[30] which operate under very trying conditions all the time and yet manage to have fewer than their fair share of accidents. HROs include power grid dispatching centers, air traffic control systems, nuclear aircraft carriers, nuclear power generating plants, hospital emergency departments, wildland firefighting crews, aircraft operations, and accident investigation teams. The better of these organizations rarely fail even though they encounter numerous unexpected events. They face an "excess" of unexpected events because their technologies are complex, their constituencies are varied, and the people who run these systems have an incomplete understanding of the systems and what they face. HROs are not magic. But they are deliberate in their attempts to deal with such problems.

We attribute the success of HROs in managing the unexpected to their determined efforts to act *mindfully*. By this we mean that they organize themselves in such a way that they are better able to notice the unexpected in the making and halt its development. If they have difficulty halting the development of the unexpected, they focus on containing it. And if the unexpected breaks through the containment, they focus on resilience and swift restoration of system functioning.

By *mindful*, we also mean striving to maintain an underlying style of mental functioning that is distinguished by continuous updating and deepening of increasingly plausible interpretations of the context, what problems define it, and what remedies it contains. The big difference between functioning in HROs and in other organizations is often most evident in the early stages when the unexpected gives off only weak signals of trouble. The overwhelming tendency is to respond to weak signals with a weak response. Mindfulness preserves the capability to see the significance of weak signals and to respond vigorously.

What Can We Learn from People Who Face Catastrophe?

HROs may seem exotic and of little practical interest because their stakes are so high and their losses can occasionally include actual loss of life. Of course, other losses—of assets, careers, reputations, legitimacy, credibility, support, trust, or goodwill—can be devastating, too, and result from unexpected events. But a loss of any kind is an outcome, and outcomes are *not* what is of primary interest to us about HROs or, in a sense, to the HROs themselves. What matters instead are their practices. Those practices produce reliable, mindful, flexible functioning because they convert concerns about failure, simplicity, operations, resilience, and expertise into routines that reduce and mitigate misspecificiation, misestimation, and misunderstanding.[31] In other words, they struggle to maintain continuing alertness to the unexpected in the face of pressure to take cognitive shortcuts. Shortcuts stem from prior success, simplifications, strategies, plans, and the use of hierarchy to pass responsibility upward. Brutal audits lie in the path of those same shortcuts.

One source of misunderstanding about the relevance of HROs to non-HROs involves a misunderstanding of issues of scale. If the activity being observed is an assembly line, for example, an unexpected shutdown is not a severe crisis (there was no fatality). But it is a crisis relative to what the supervisor expected would not fail and a crisis relative to precautions taken so that it wouldn't fail. A visit from the Securities and Exchange Commission to a CEO's office does not produce fatalities, but it can affect markets, share price, and liability. In each case, the meaning of the unexpected is contextual. Once we understand the context, the precautions, the assumptions, the focus of attention, and what was ignored, it becomes clear that many organizations are just as exposed to threats as HROs are, and just as much in need of mindfulness. In all organizations, people do things that they expect to continue doing reliably and for which unexpected interruptions can eventually turn disastrous if they manage the unexpected poorly. This possibility is more at the center of attention for HROs than for most other organizations. But it is a possibility that haunts all organizations.

All organizations, not just HROs, develop culturally accepted beliefs about the world and its hazards. All organizations develop precautionary norms that are set out in regulations, procedures, rules, guidelines, job descriptions, and training materials, as well as informally on the grapevine. And all organizations accumulate unnoticed events that are at odds with accepted beliefs about hazards.[32] It is similarities such as these that warrant transfer of the lessons from HROs to other organizations. For example, HROs develop complex beliefs about the world and revise these beliefs, but they revise them more often than most other organizations. Likewise, HROs develop precautionary norms just like everyone else. But unlike everyone else, they use both small failures and the liabilities of success as inputs when they develop these precautions. And like all organizations, HROs accumulate unnoticed events that are at odds with what they expected. But they also tend to notice these accumulating events sooner, when they are smaller. Each of these elaborations of the basics by HROs suggests directions in which other organizations can make their own elaborations in the interest of heightened mindfulness.

The environment of HROs is one in which there are high-risk technologies. These technologies must be mastered by means other than trial-and-error learning, since in many cases the first error will also be the last trial. HRO environments unfold rapidly, and errors propagate quickly. Understanding is never perfect, and people are under pressure to make wise choices with insufficient information. But whose environment isn't like this? In fact, you could say that how well or how poorly people manage the unexpected is a fundamental issue that underlies the handling of any pressing business problem. Thus the difference between an HRO and a non-HRO is not as large as it might appear. In both settings, trouble starts small and is signaled by weak symptoms that are easy to miss, especially when expectations are strong and mindfulness is weak. These small discrepancies can cumulate, expand, and have disproportionately large consequences. This path of development is also similar across organizations. What differs across organizations are variables such as how much value people place on catching such developments earlier rather than later, how much knowledge people have of the system and its capacity to detect and remedy early indications of trouble, and how much support there is from top management to allocate resources to early detection and management of the unexpected, error-acknowledging communication, and commitment to mindfulness at all levels.

Chapter Summary

Unexpected events can get you into trouble unless you create a mindful infrastructure that continually tracks small failures, resists oversimplification, is sensitive to operations, maintains capabilities for resilience, and monitors shifting locations of expertise. When these five principles are violated, as they were by the system that was built to manage the Cerro Grande prescribed burn, people fall back on practices that deny small failures, accept simple diagnoses, take frontline operations for granted, overlook capabilities for resilience, and defer to authorities rather than experts. In the early stages of the Cerro Grande burn, personnel realistically expected that the burn plan was doable, resources were sufficient, the dispatch system was responsive, and the weather conditions were acceptable. However, as the prescribed burn became unexpectedly more active and complex, small misjudgments grew into larger problems that were easy to detect but hard to solve. This progression is not unique to wildland firefighting, however. We find failures of expectations everywhere, which is why managing the unexpected is so crucial.

Lessons concerning ways to cope with the unexpected were drawn from high reliability organizations (HROs). The best of these organizations operate under trying conditions all the time and yet manage to have fewer than their fair share of accidents. These trying conditions stem from complex technologies, contentious constituencies, and managers and operators who have an incomplete understanding of their own systems and what they face. Success in working under these conditions is due in part to mindful organizing that allows people to notice the unexpected in the making, halt it or contain it, and restore system functioning. The hallmark of an HRO is not that it is error-free but that errors do not disable it.

In Chapter Two, we take a closer look at the foundations of resilient, reliable functioning, namely, the nature of expectations and unexpected events and the ways in which a general capability for mindful organizing halts the development of unexpected events. After that, we examine the specifics of mindful organizing, focusing on three principles of anticipation that involve failures, simplification, and operations in Chapter Three and then on two principles of containment that involve resilience and expertise in Chapter Four. In the final three chapters, we discuss audits, culture changes, and managerial practices that can lead to more mindful organized action.

2

Expectations
and Mindfulness

If you want to manage the unexpected, you have to understand, first, how expectations work and, second, how to engage them mindfully. Those two topics are the focus of this chapter. The basic argument is that expectations are built into organizational roles, routines, and strategies. These expectations create the orderliness and predictability that we count on when we organize. Expectations, however, are a mixed blessing because they create blind spots. Blind spots sometimes take the form of belated recognition of unexpected, threatening events. And frequently blind spots get larger simply because we do a biased search for evidence that confirms the accuracy of our original expectations. The problem with blind spots is that they often conceal small errors that are getting bigger and can produce disabling brutal audits. To counteract these blind spots, organizations try to develop a greater awareness of discriminatory detail. This enriched awareness, which we call mindfulness, uncovers early signs that expectations are inadequate, that unexpected events are unfolding, and that recovery needs to be implemented. Recovery requires updating both of one's understanding of what is happening and of the lines of action that were tied to the earlier expectations.

The close ties among the expected, the unexpected, and mindful organizing are clearly visible in the resilient performance of flight operations on the deck of an aircraft carrier. Aircraft carriers have been a prototype of high reliability systems almost from the beginning.[1] Therefore, we use carriers as our example throughout this chapter for historical reasons as well as because their practices transfer readily to other settings such as health care.

People who work on carriers spend much of their time on a flat deck that has been called "the most dangerous 4½ acres in the world." Here's how one Navy veteran describes life on a carrier:

> Imagine that it's a busy day, and you shrink San Francisco airport to only one short runway and one ramp and one gate. Make planes take off and land at the same time, at half the present time interval, rock the runway from side to side, and require that everyone who leaves in the morning returns the same day. Make sure the equipment is so close to the envelope that it's fragile. Then turn off the radar to avoid detection, impose strict controls on the radios, fuel the aircraft in place with their engines running, put an enemy in the air, and scatter live bombs and rockets around. Now wet the whole thing down with sea water and oil, and man it with twenty-year-olds, half of whom have never seen an airplane close-up. Oh, and by the way, try not to kill anyone.[2]

Can you think of another environment that is quite this full of expectations and demands for mindful action? Here are some examples of those expectations: team members expect that a signal intended to alter a flight path will be followed, that a flight crew will be rested, that situation assessments are shared, that the correct weapons are loaded onto aircraft, that fuel is not contaminated, that weather forecasts are accurate, that there is space available on the deck to move aircraft, and that operators know their jobs. The unexpected in carrier operations occurs in three different forms: sometimes expected events don't materialize, sometimes unexpected events do materialize, and sometimes the unimaginable appears like a bolt out of the blue. The system built around flight operations on a carrier strives for mindful organizing in order to increase alertness and reduce the disruption caused by unexpected events. Alertness can be compromised by expectations. And mindfulness alerts people to potential trouble spots.

Expectations and the Search for Confirmation

To have an expectation is to envision something, usually for good reasons, that is reasonably certain to come about.[3] To expect something is to be mentally ready for it. Every deliberate action you take is based on assumptions about how the world will react to what you do. "Expectancies form the basis for virtually all deliberate actions because expectancies about how the world operates serve as implicit assumptions that guide behavioral choices."[4] Expectations provide a significant infrastructure for everyday life. They are like a routine that suggests the probable course of events. They direct your attention to certain features of events, which means that they affect what you notice, mull over, and remember. When you expect that something will happen, that is a lot like testing a hypothesis.

For example, if you expect that a bolt left on a carrier deck is no big deal, that's a hypothesis that nothing bad will result from leaving one lying around. If that stray bolt is ingested into a jet engine and the engine explodes (which has actually happened during carrier deployments), your hypothesis is proved wrong, the expectation is disconfirmed, and you and your system have a chance to learn a lesson, albeit the hard way. In fact, crews on carriers have learned from this explosion. They now conduct foreign-object damage (FOD) walkdowns several times a day. Everyone, regardless of rank, walks the full length of the deck and picks up anything that might be sucked into an engine. The FOD walkdown is a microcosm of how expectations function, how they can produce blind spots, and how their disconfirmation can be the basis for both serious problems and learning.

Many of your expectations are reasonably accurate. They tend to be confirmed, partly because they are based on your experience and partly because you correct those that have negative consequences. The tricky part is that all of us tend to be awfully generous in what we accept as evidence that our expectations are confirmed.[5] Furthermore, we actively seek out evidence that confirms our expectations and avoid evidence that disconfirms them. For example, if you ex-pect that Navy aviators are brash, you'll tend to do a biased search for indications of brashness whenever you spot an aviator.[6] You're less likely to do a more balanced search in which you weigh all the evidence and look just as closely for disconfirming evidence in the form of aviator behavior that is tentative and modest. This biased search sets at least two problems in motion. First, you overlook ac-cumulating evidence that events are not developing as you thought they would. Second, you tend to overestimate the validity of your expectations. Both tendencies become even stronger if you are under pressure. As pressure increases, people are more likely to search for confirming information and to ignore information that is inconsistent with their expectations.[7]

People also search for confirmation in other forms of expecting such as routines and plans. Organizations often presume that be-cause they have routines to deal with problems, this proves that they understand those problems. Although there is a grain of truth to that inference, what they fail to see is that their routines are also expectations that are subject to the very same traps as any other ex-pectations. Whenever a routine is activated, people assume that the world today is pretty much like the world that existed at the time the routine was first learned. Furthermore, people tend to look for confirmation that their existing routines are correct. And over time, they come to see more and more confirmation based on fewer and fewer data. What is missing are continuing efforts to update the rou-tines and expectations and to act in ways that would compel such updating.

This same pattern of confirmation seeking is associated with plans. Plans guide people to search narrowly for confirmation that the plans are correct. Disconfirming evidence is avoided, and plans lure you into overlooking a buildup of the unexpected. This is not surprising since much of the imagery used to describe plans is simi-lar to the imagery people use when they talk about expectations. Earlier we said that expectations could be understood as assump-tions that guide choices, as suggestions of how the world will react to your actions, and as hypotheses waiting to be tested. If you understand the problems that expectations create, you understand the problems that plans create. And you may begin to understand why a preoccupation with plans and planning makes it tough for you to act mindfully.

People in HROs work hard to counteract the tendency to seek confirmation by designing practices that incorporate the five principles. They understand that their expectations are incomplete and that they can come closer to getting it right if they doubt those expectations that seem to be confirmed most often.[8] For example, landing-signal officers, who guide pilots onto the carrier deck in their last few seconds of flight, assume that pilots are coolheaded, are not prone to panic, and wouldn't be flying onto a carrier if the opposite were true. And yet these officers also know that seasoned pilots can sometimes lose their cool when, for example, they get disoriented at night, can't distinguish between the black sky and the black sea, and unexpectedly lose altitude while circling to dump excess fuel. If landing officers expect that a pilot is calm, they nonetheless make an intentional effort to pick up signs of lack of calm (in other words, they fight their own expectations). They often listen even more closely to the quality of the pilot's voice to detect subtle cues of tension that suggest that this particular nighttime recovery may be going sour.

The tendencies to seek confirmation and avoid disconfirmation are well-honed, well-practiced human tendencies. That's why HROs have to work so hard and so continuously to *override* these tendencies and remain alert. And that's why you may have to work just as hard. All of us face an ongoing struggle for alertness because we face an ongoing preference for information that confirms.

The Nature of Unexpected Events

Unexpected events can take one of three forms. The first form of the unexpected occurs when an event that was expected to happen fails to occur. For example, fatigue is an issue on aircraft carriers, and everyone recognizes it. It is not uncommon during high-tempo periods for people to be on duty for twenty hours, off for four, and back on for twenty. The expectation is that fatigued crews will perform more poorly than fresh crews. The surprise in all of this is that the expected deterioration in performance often fails to materialize. Fatigued crews have worked together, know each other's quirks, accommodate them, and perform well as a unit. Fresh crews, people who are relative strangers to one another, often have to work out their coordination and rhythms and are rusty at the beginning of their shift. It takes time to develop smooth coordination, so performance is below average early in the shift and gets better as the shift progresses.

A second form of the unexpected occurs when an event that was not expected to happen does happen. For example, it is expected that pilots will occasionally miss the arresting wires when they try to land on a carrier deck (this is called a bolter). When a pilot bolters, this interrupts the smooth functioning of the system while that person circles around for a second and sometimes a third try. It would be unexpected if several people boltered on the same day or if several people in the same squadron did so. It would be a lot harder to blame a cluster of bolters on simple pilot error. The alternative diagnosis of system error is more troubling and a much bigger threat to the captain's bottom line of full readiness to engage the enemy.

The third form of the unexpected occurs when an event that was simply unthought of happens. For example, carrier personnel never imagined that women pilots would be added to crews that had been an all-male stronghold for decades. No one expected this, and it made no sense. Federal law precluded women from flying combat missions, there was no improvement in readiness or economic advantage gained by assigning the small number of women jet pilots to extended cruises, women pilots had not previously been trained to deploy in fleet squadrons, there were few women qualified to fly off ships, and the casual atmosphere of the ready room on the ship sometimes led to more tension in crew relationships when women used the same facilities. Against this background, the jolt felt when a plane landed on the deck and a woman pilot stepped out of the cockpit is hard to overstate.

In each of these three cases, the surprise starts with an expectation. People start with expectations that fatigue reduces coordination, faulty landings are rare events, and aircraft carriers are ships staffed by men. Presumably, if you hold these expectations, you look for evidence that confirms them rather than evidence that disconfirms them. If you find confirming evidence, this "proves" that your hunches about the world are accurate, that you are in control, that you know what's up, and that you are safe. The continuing search for confirming evidence postpones your realization that your model has its limits. If you are slow to realize that things are not the way you expected them to be, the problem worsens and becomes harder to solve and gets entangled with other problems. When it finally becomes clear that your expectation is wrong, there may be few options left to resolve the problem. In the meantime, efficiency and effectiveness have declined, the system is now vulnerable to further collapse, and safety, reputations, and production are in jeopardy.

A significant goal of HROs is to increase their understanding of the third form of the unexpected and to expand knowledge of "the imagined deemed possible."[9] HRO principles steer people toward mindful practices that encourage imagination. The crucial nature of imagination is reflected, as you may recall, in the report of the commission investigating the terrorist attacks on September 11, 2001. It found shortfalls in imagination prior to the collapse of the twin towers. The commission's report contains this striking assertion: "Imagination is not a gift usually associated with bureaucracies. . . . It is therefore crucial to find a way of routinizing, even bureaucratizing the exercise of imagination. Doing so requires more than finding an expert who can imagine that aircraft could be used as weapons."[10] It takes more than a shrewd expert to forestall the unexpected in most situations. It takes mindful practices that encourage imagination, foster enriched expectations, raise doubts about all expectations, increase the ability to make novel sense of

small interruptions in expectations, and facilitate learning that in-
tensifies and deepens alertness. We will say more about these mindful practices shortly.

People sometimes inadvertently trivialize the importance of
imagination. For example, these days we keep hearing the hollow
maxim "Expect the unexpected." That well-meaning sentiment assumes that people can live their lives while assuming that their
expectations are misleading. The problem is, they can't afford to.
They live, instead, as if their expectations are basically correct and
as if there is little that can surprise them. To do otherwise would be
to forgo any feeling of control or predictability.

That's why managing the unexpected is much harder than it
may seem. People in HROs worry a lot about the temptation to
treat unexpected events as if they were really no big deal. Sociologist Diane Vaughan found this tendency to "normalize" the unexpected in her reanalysis of the 1986 NASA *Challenger* disaster.
When unexpected burn marks appeared on the O-rings that sealed
sections of the booster rockets, engineers changed their definition
of what was an "acceptable risk." They now claimed that it was
acceptable for hot gases to leak past the gaskets. What they first
treated as an unexpected event they now treated as an expected
event. This was not the first such redefinition of acceptable risk.
The judgment of what was "normal" went from the judgment that
it was normal to have heat on the primary O-ring to that it was
normal to have erosion on the primary O-ring to that it was normal
to have gas blowby to that it was normal to have blowby reaching
the secondary O-ring and finally to the judgment that it was normal
to have erosion on the secondary ring.[11] The words of NASA's
Larry Wear say it all:

> Once you've accepted an anomaly or something less than perfect,
> you know, you've given up your virginity. You can't go back. You're
> at the point that it's very hard to draw the line. You know, next time
> they say it's the same problem, it's just eroded 5 mils more. Once you
> accepted it, where do you draw the line? Once you've done it, it's

very difficult to go back now and get very hard-nosed and say I'm not going to accept that.[12]

The moral is that perceptions of the unexpected are fleeting. When people are interrupted, they tend to be candid about what happened for a short period of time, and then they get their stories straight in ways that justify their actions and protect their reputations. And when official stories get straightened out, learning stops. This mechanism is described in a colorful manner by historians who have studied mistakes in the military:

> In the chaos of the battlefield there is the tendency of all ranks to combine and recast the story of their achievements into a shape which shall satisfy the susceptibilities of national and regimental vain-glory. . . . On the actual day of battle naked truths may be picked up for the asking. But by the following morning they have already begun to get into their uniforms.[13]

You'll probably know when something unexpected happens because you'll feel surprised, puzzled, or anxious. Aviators call these feelings *leemers* (probably derived from *leery*), the feeling that something is not quite right, but you can't put your finger on it. Trust those feelings. They are a solid clue that your model of the world is in error. More important, try to hold on to those feelings and resist the temptation to gloss over what has just happened and treat it as normal. In that brief interval between surprise and successful normalizing lies one of your few opportunities to discover what you don't know. This is one of those rare moments when you can significantly improve your understanding. If you wait too long, normalizing will take over, and you'll be convinced that there is nothing to learn. Most opportunities for learning come in the form of brief moments. And one of the best moments for learning, a moment of the unexpected, is also one of the shortest-lived moments. People in HROs try to freeze and stretch out their unexpected moments in order to learn more from them.

The Idea of Mindfulness

By now it should be clear that it pays to be aware of your expectations. Expectations act like an invisible hand that guides you toward soothing perceptions that confirm your hunches and away from more troublesome ones that don't. But it is those very same troublesome perceptions that foreshadow the unexpected. If you depend too much on a simple set of expectations, unusual events can develop to more serious levels before you even notice them. People in HROs try to weaken the grip of this invisible hand of expectations so that they can see more, make better sense of what they see, and remain more attuned to their current situation. They do this by attending to at least the five principles described in Chapter One: preoccupation with failure, reluctance to simplify, sensitivity to operations, commitment to resilience, and deference to expertise. These principles can influence the design of processes and move the system toward what we have called a state of mindfulness.

Formally, we define *mindfulness* as "a rich awareness of discriminatory detail." By that we mean that when people act, they are aware of context, of ways in which details differ (in other words, they discriminate among details), and of deviations from their expectations. Mindful people have the "big picture," but it is a big picture of the moment. This is sometimes called situation awareness,[14] but we use that concept sparingly. Mindfulness is different from situation awareness in the sense that it involves the combination of ongoing scrutiny of existing expectations, continuous refinement and differentiation of expectations based on newer experiences, willingness and capability to invent new expectations that make sense of unprecedented events, a more nuanced appreciation of context and ways to deal with it, and identification of new dimensions of context that improve foresight and current functioning.[15]

Mindfulness is about the quality of attention. HROs become more vulnerable to error when their attention is distracted, unstable, and dominated by abstractions. All three of these predispose people to misestimate, misunderstand, and misspecify what they think they face.[16] Distractions often take the form of associative thinking ("That reminds me of the time when . . ."), which draws attention away from the present and from an awareness of change and substitutes abstract ideas for concrete details.

Mindfulness is focused on clear and detailed comprehension of emerging threats and on factors that interfere with such comprehension. Small failures have to be noticed (the principle of preoccupation with failure), and their distinctiveness must be retained rather than lost in a category (reluctance to simplify). People need to remain aware of ongoing operations if they want to notice nuances that could be symptoms of failure (sensitivity to operations). Attention is also crucial for locating pathways to recovery (commitment to resilience) and the knowledge of how to implement those pathways (deference to expertise). Faced with such demands, mindful organizations devote more time than other organizations to examining failure as a window on the health of the system, resisting the urge to simplify assumptions about the world, observing operations and their effects, developing resilience to manage unexpected events, and identifying local experts and creating a climate of deference to them.

Consider the *Columbia* space shuttle accident that claimed the lives of seven astronauts.[17] Careless use of categories contributed to the disaster. NASA makes a distinction between problems that are "in-family" and those that are "out-of-family." An in-family event is "a reportable problem that was previously experienced, analyzed, and understood."[18] There are two key phrases in that definition: "reportable problems" and "previously experienced." If you want to report something, you need to have words and categories at hand to do the reporting. And those very words can limit what you see and report. Whatever labels a group uses will color what members of the group think they see and report. This means that people may miss the unexpected and label too many events as "in-family." This happens simply because you have to use words that have established meanings to report those unexpected events. And that's where mindfulness comes in.

Mindfulness is important because it weakens the tendency to simplify occurrences into familiar events (the tendency to normalize) and strengthens the tendency to redefine the event into something that is less familiar. Less mindful practice normalizes; more mindful practice anomalizes—and by *anomalize*, we mean that mindfulness captures unique features that slow the speed with which details are normalized. These visible anomalies foreshadow potential problems and opportunities and reduce the tendency to incubate events until they become unmanageable.

Mindfulness involves strengthening the capabilities to hold on to the object being perceived, to prevent the mind from wandering off that object and being distracted, and to render observations more vivid and more detailed. The intent is to strengthen nonforgetfulness and exclude anything that hinders a calmer mind. Mindfulness has "the characteristic of not wobbling, [of] not floating away from the object. Its function is absence of confusion or non-forgetfulness."[19] When the mind "wobbles," it flies off from the current task in a flurry of conceptual associations, and may not be pulled back to the task before problems have already been set in motion.

Here's an example from nuclear power generation as described by a former admiral in the Navy:

> I see events and incidents as an attitude problem, but the attitude may be due to disruption or distraction. In the navy, I insisted that any watch stander be diligent about his duties. I didn't tolerate distractions—telephone calls, people wandering up to ask about the weather. In industry the watch supervisor in the control room is filling out paperwork, having discussions with others, people calling to find out where someone is. I want to correlate distractions to questionable actions. Was there a distraction? People don't deliberately make mistakes. There must have been a distraction.[20]

The admiral goes on to suggest that managers should list "the distractions today" every morning. If peer review teams or reengineering consultants will be visiting or if new competitive threats have materialized overnight, people need to know that. They need to be alerted that their attention may wander and that continuing efforts will be necessary to bring it back to the task. For those with well-developed skills of mindfulness, daily distractions will not be a big problem. For the rest of us, distractions could produce an inadvertent lapse that escalates into the equivalent of an escaped fire. In this context, the key questions, for individuals and systems alike, are "Am I able to concentrate to remove distractions so that I can focus calmly?" and "Do I return quickly to my task when my mind wanders?"

Mindfulness, finally, is about the ability of a system to concentrate on what is going on here and now. Sure, managers have memories based on previous events and bold plans about future events. But past experiences and future intentions are influential only in the sense that they materialize and are expressed in the *current* moment. For example, memories of earlier aircraft carrier deployments and plans for the future missions are nothing more than thoughts that can draw attention away from the current job of signaling pilots who are trying to land on a carrier whose deck is rolling in heavy seas. Even if the memories consist of prior experiences with tricky landings, those memories are simplified in hindsight to suit the current context and may mislead the person giving the landing signals.

Mindfulness in Carrier Operations

We have discussed separately the notions of expectations, the unexpected, and mindfulness. These three are tied together by five principles of mindfulness that involve failure, simplification, operations, resilience, and expertise. These principles counteract the blind spots created by expectations because they enable local practices to capture discriminatory details that foreshadow the unexpected. This complex pattern is found in many of the more successful reliability-seeking organizations that strive for resilient performance.

We can see this pattern if we take a closer look at reliable organizing in carrier operations. We want to emphasize that the problems of a carrier are similar to the problems you face. At the most basic level, the task of people on a carrier is to move aircraft off the pointed end of the ship and back onto the blunt end of the ship. And at the most basic level, your task is to move products or services out the front door and raw materials in the back door. Carrier personnel have to transform the raw materials of new recruits, fickle technology, and unreliable aircraft into total readiness, just as you have to transform your raw materials into something that is better than what your competitors have to offer. Carrier personnel add value and achieve victory. You add value and achieve market share. Carriers have to live within budgets, and so do you. On carriers, budgets for aviation fuel are sometimes cut. As a result, pilots get less practice at difficult night landings, which can cause serious trouble down the line. Pleas from the captain up through the chain of command do not necessarily bring relief and more money. And your pleas often meet a similar fate. People on carriers pay close attention to how often pilots achieve their goal of a perfect landing and snag the third arresting wire with their tailhook. By comparison, you pay attention to very different standards to measure performance, standards such as inventory turn, sales in the most recent quarter, or volume of customer complaints. Your world and the world of a carrier may look very different, but you both are trying to gauge the health of your systems. Both of you are trying to discover clear criteria of performance, while you also try to remain alert, avoid complacency, learn from failures, and cope with whatever is thrown at you.

Because the issues you face in common can be managed by implementing the same HRO principles, we conclude the chapter by showing how personnel on carriers convert principles of reliable functioning into practices that produce wariness, concentration, and awareness. Recall the enormous potential for trouble on a carrier. It is not just that you have six thousand people crammed into tight spaces away from shore on an 1,100-foot, 95,000-ton floating city run by an overburdened "mayor." It is also the fact that within those tight spaces, you also have people working with jet aircraft, jet fuel, nuclear reactors, nuclear weapons, an onboard air traffic control system, refueling and resupply from adjacent ships that are moving, and a surrounding battle group of seven to nine ships that are supposed to protect the carrier but can themselves also be dangerous obstacles in fog, high seas, or unpredictable weather. But there is order amid this chaos. And much of that order comes from practices that institutionalize mindfulness. These practices are based on the same five principles of mindfulness that we find in other HROs.

The Principles at Work

First, people on carriers are *preoccupied with failure*. Every landing is graded, and the grades are used to improve performance. Every landing is also televised throughout the ship so that everyone sees how everyone else performs. Near misses are debriefed within the hour, and everyone is required to write down what they saw and heard prior to the incident. Small failures such as a plane in the wrong position on a full deck or a pilot's continued inability to snag the third arresting wire when landing are treated as signs of potential larger problems within the system, such as poor communication among deck handlers or inadequate training for the Air Wing (the aviation equivalent of an infantry division).

Second, people on carriers are *reluctant to simplify*. They take nothing for granted. They do not assume that any aircraft is ready for launch until it has been checked in multiple ways by redundant inspections. Hand signals, voice signals, and colored uniforms are used to convey information about who is responsible for what. If a pilot whose plane is positioned on a catapult for launch is then told to reduce engine power, he won't do it for fear of being launched at reduced power into the ocean. He keeps full power on until the catapult officer walks directly in front of his plane, stands directly over the 2 million–horsepower catapult, and signals that he should reduce power. Of course, the catapult officer will not stand there until he visually confirms that the catapult is safe and can't be fired while he's standing in its path.

Third, people on carriers maintain continuous *sensitivity to operations*. Officers from the captain on down are in continuous communication during flight operations and exchange information about the status of the activity. The entire ship is attuned to launching and recovering aircraft. The captain, who is in charge of the carrier, and the commander of the Air Wing, who is in charge of the aircraft, are positioned physically to observe all steps of the operations. Insensitivity to operations was clearly evident in one near miss that could have been catastrophic. The carrier was running at high speed in heavy seas when a request was made that it slow down so that aircraft could be moved from the flight deck down to the hangar deck by means of an elevator that is on the edge of the deck and exposed to the sea. The ship had other priorities and did not slow down immediately. Growing impatient and thinking the seas had calmed down, the deck officer ordered the elevator lowered. Seven men and an aircraft were washed overboard. All were rescued, itself an amazing feat.

Fourth, people on carriers have a *commitment to resilience*. Crews know the importance of routines and predictable behavior. They also know that no one understands the technology, the situation, or the people completely, so surprises are inevitable. And with surprise comes the necessity to improvise, think on your feet, and contain and bounce back from unexpected events. For example, when Dick Martin, the first captain of the carrier *Carl Vinson*, found himself in an intense storm off the coast of Virginia in 1983, the winds were so strong that he improvised by driving the carrier at 10 knots *in reverse* in order to reduce the speed of the winds across the deck and allow the aircraft to land more safely. Gene Rochlin describes a planned launch involving both precise timing and all of the aircraft on deck. The first aircraft to be put on the catapult malfunctioned and could not be cleared from the catapult. The entire launch plan had to be reconfigured with new strategies for the raid and new emergency fields. The reconfiguration was finished in less than ten minutes.[21]

And fifth, people on carriers maintain *deference to expertise*. The boss of an air squadron who knows the quirks of his own pilots may momentarily override higher-ranking officers in the tower and decide how planes will be landed when a member of his squadron loses hydraulics while attempting to land.

Mindfulness and Safe Operations

Despite their success in avoiding costly mistakes, no one on a carrier understands carrier operations perfectly or with complete certainty. And the same holds true for any HRO. Puzzlement is certainly common in any organization you've ever been part of. What this means is that it is impossible to manage any organization solely by means of mindless control systems that depend on rules, plans, routines, stable categories, and fixed criteria for correct performance. No one knows enough to design such a system so that it can cope with a dynamic environment. Instead, designers who want to hold dynamic systems together have to organize in ways that evoke mindful work. People have to adopt a style of mental functioning that enables continuous learning as well as ongoing refinement of expectations. Carriers are guided as much by updated expectations as they are by stable computations.

At the start of this chapter, we mentioned the surprising fact that the way people work on carriers is a lot like the way people work in health care settings. This link suggests how you can generalize carrier practices to your own firm. The influential report on medical errors developed by the Institute of Medicine had this to say about the relevance of carriers and their environments to health care.

> [Health care] is very different from a manufacturing process, mostly because of huge variability in patients and circumstances, the need to adapt processes quickly, the rapidly changing knowledge base, and the importance of highly trained professionals who must use expert judgment in dynamic settings. . . . The performance of crews and

flight personnel on aircraft carriers provides an example that has features that are closer to those in health care environments than manufacturing. On an aircraft carrier, fueling aircraft and loading munitions are examples of the risks posed when performing incompatible activities in close proximity. On the flight deck, 100 to 200 people fuel, load munitions, and maintain aircraft that take off and are recovered at 48- to 60-second intervals. . . . [These flight operations are] an example of organizational performance requiring nearly continuous operational reliability despite complex interrelated patterns among many people. These activities cannot be fully mapped out beforehand because of changes in weather (e.g. wind direction and strength), sea conditions, time of day and visibility, returning aircraft arrivals, and so forth. Yet, surprisingly, generally mapped out sequences can be carried out with very high reliability in novel situations using improvisation and adaptation and personnel who are highly trained but not highly educated. . . . As in health care, it is not possible in such dynamic settings to anticipate and write a rule for every circumstance. Once-rigid orders that prescribed how to perform each operation have been replaced by more flexible, less hierarchical methods. For example, although the captain's commands usually take precedence, junior officers can, and do, change these priorities when they believe that following an order will risk the crew's safety. Such an example demonstrates that even in technologically sophisticated, hazardous, and unpredictable environments it is possible to foster real-time problem solving and to institute safety systems that incorporate a knowledge of human factors.[22]

Mindfulness is crucial for carriers, hospitals, investment banks, or firefighting teams because reliability and safe operations have such an odd configuration. Safe, reliable performance "is a dynamic non-event—what produces the stable outcome is constant change rather than continuous repetition. To achieve this stability, a change in one system parameter must be compensated for by change in other parameters."[23] The problem is that when a system is operating safely and reliably, there are constant outcomes and nothing to watch. That does not mean that nothing is happening. On the contrary, there is continuous mutual adjustment. One change is compensated for by another change. The deck becomes more slippery, so the spacing between the planes must be increased. The radio signal begins to break up, so the crew resorts to hand signals. The seas get heavy, so aircraft are not moved between decks on elevators that are exposed to the sea. Armed weapons explode at different temperatures, so one person is removed from deck duty and assigned the task of recording which weapons are on which planes. In the event of a deck fire, firefighters will know which areas need immediate attention to prevent explosion.

Mutual adjustments like these preserve reliability. But they require mindful action. If you want to manage the unexpected more skillfully, you need to follow the lead of carriers where significant effort is invested in mindfulness and significant penalties are assessed for mindlessness.

Chapter Summary

When people form expectations, they assume that certain sequences of action are likely to happen. These assumptions, which are embedded in routines, rules, norms, training, and roles, establish orderly guides for performance and interpretation. However, the same expectations that produce order and efficiency can also undermine reliable, resilient performance because they encourage confirmation seeking, reliance on existing categories, and simplification. Undermining instances result in unexpected and unimagined events that grow in complexity and can endanger operations the longer they remain unnoticed. The liabilities of expectations can be countered by practices that produce awareness of discriminatory details that are relevant to failure, simplification, operations, resilience, and expertise. Awareness improves when attention is not distracted, is focused on the here and now, is able to hold on to the problem of interest, is wary of preexisting categories, and is committed to implementation of the five principles. This pattern of awareness and attention is called mindfulness. This pattern has been observed in flight operations on carrier decks as well as in other settings where reliable performance is sustained under trying conditions. To manage the unexpected, organizations need to assess candidly the expectations that hold them together, the grounds on which they believe these expectations, the things these expectations keep them from seeing, and their capability for mindful engagement with these expectations. Mindful engagement is built around five principles that have been inducted from observations of high reliability functioning. These principles fall into two clusters: principles of anticipation (failure, simplification, operations) and principles of containment (resilience, expertise). In Chapters Three and Four, we discuss each set of principles in greater detail.

3

The Three Principles
of Anticipation

In this chapter and the next, we take a closer look at the five principles that enable HROs to maintain reliable performance while dealing with the unexpected. In this chapter, we examine the first three principles, all having to do with anticipation. As we noted earlier, the five principles serve as a basis for reasoning and a guide for conduct in high reliability systems. They also provide a framework for other organizations as well. In Chapter Two, we focused on one kind of HRO, the aircraft carrier, and used it to illustrate how effective performance is influenced by the expected, the unexpected, and mindfulness. Here and in Chapter Four, we use a different kind of HRO, nuclear power plants, to illustrate principles that create mindfulness.[1]

Everyone can see that nuclear power generation is a complex and hazardous technology.[2] What everyone cannot see is how daunting an administrative and organizational task it is to manage nuclear power plants safely. The challenge is partly tied to the complexity of the environment. Many nonrepetitive tasks are concentrated in an environment made dangerous by temperature, pressures, fluids, mechanical power, electricity, and the sheer weight of the equipment. A nuclear plant is safest when it is running, which means that maintaining the capability for safe shutdown and startup without uncontrolled radioactivity release are the central concerns.[3] Complex though these systems are, they are not all that different from the complex systems you face. Anthropologist Constance Perin describes organizational complexity as an "infrastructure of conundrums." She means by this that "paradoxes, dilemmas, and contradictions appear often enough in technology-driven enterprises to warrant being re-understood as *expectable* outcroppings of complexity. To 'manage' a complex system is to keep untying the knots it can get itself into."[4] The main problem in complex systems is that designers and operators know much about the technology's inner workings and its operating environment, but they also know that they have not imagined, deduced, or experienced all of the ways it can generate unexpected events.

One example of a dilemma in nuclear plants involves staffing. "To keep radiation doses within acceptable levels, health physicists ask for shorter periods of work from a larger pool of people; that raises costs, which may adversely affect corporate . . . market standing."[5] Furthermore, when extra people need to be hired for maintenance during outages, there is pressure to produce a huge number of security checks quickly in order to avoid people sitting around.[6] Bringing people in at the last minute is risky but cheap. Trade-offs like this produce an infrastructure of conundrums.

As we examine reliable organizing in nuclear power generation, keep two things in mind. First, *coordination and information are crucial*. "The crux of reactor control is . . . keeping track of expectable interactions within a complicated, often opaque system and responding promptly to those not expected. Close coordination among many specialists' perspectives and knowledge is key."[7]

Second, *the main product in nuclear power generation is not what you think it is*. The mistakes that managers dare not make involve trust, not the interruption of electricity. "A station's primary product is a cultural commodity: civic and market trust in its managers' and experts' competencies."[8] Profitable production of electricity is secondary to establishing and sustaining that trust. Without trust, there is no production. Implementation of principles associated with reliable anticipation and reliable containment are the means to preserve that trust.

An Overview of Anticipation

Earlier we noted that the shopworn admonition "Expect the unexpected" has lost some of its meaning. The Centers for Disease Control and Prevention (CDC) have improved on this expression. In a document titled "Preventing Emerging Infectious Diseases: A Strategy for the 21st Century," the CDC noted, "Because we do not know what new diseases will arise, we must always *be prepared for the unexpected*."[9] Preparing for the unexpected involves more than merely expecting it. That "more than" forms the basis of the first three HRO principles. Specifically, anticipation means mindful attention to three things: failure, simplification, and operations. To anticipate is to foresee or imagine an eventual unchecked outcome, based on small disparities. Frequently such sensing means taking a small cue and imagining a scenario in which this single small marker is the sign of a larger, more harrowing situation.[10] Anticipation, however, is not just an exercise in sensing; it is also an exercise in stopping the development of undesirable events. The escalation and spread of small discrepancies are slowed by actions of anticipation and stopped by actions of containment.

Some experts argue that it is impossible to anticipate the unexpected both because there are almost an infinite number of weak signals in the environment and because the ability to pick up these weak signals is far beyond the existing technological capabilities of most organizations.[11] Yet organizations that persistently have less than their fair share of accidents seem to be better able to sense significant unexpected events than organizations that have more accidents. Members of HROs don't necessarily see discrepancies any more quickly, but when they do spot discrepancies, they understand their meaning more fully and can deal with them more confidently. This ability to become aware of unanticipated events seems to be enhanced by practices that operationalize the first three principles of HROs: preoccupation with failure, reluctance to simplify interpretations, and sensitivity to operations. We discuss each of these three in the following sections.

Principle 1: Preoccupation with Failure

"Failure is not an option!"[12] That stirring sentiment was at the core of the successful effort to retrieve the damaged *Apollo 13* spacecraft (launched April 11, 1970, and landed six days later). Lost in all the subsequent hype of this phrase is the lesson that to avoid failure, you've first got to embrace it. That's not as crazy as it sounds. To "embrace" failure means two things for HROs. First, it means that they pay close attention to weak signals of failure that may be symptoms of larger problems within the system. Second, it means that the strategies adopted by HROs often spell out mistakes that people don't dare make. Organizations that look relentlessly for symptoms of malfunctioning, especially when these symptoms can be tied to strategic mistakes, are better able to create practices that preclude those mistakes.

Weak Signals of Failure and Nuclear Power

Let's take a closer look at the failure principle, starting with a nuclear power plant as an example. In 2002, at the Davis-Besse nuclear power plant outside Toledo, Ohio, a 6½-inch-thick metal liner designed to contain radioactive material under pressure of 2,200 pounds per square inch was found to be corroded down to the width of a pencil eraser over an oval area about 10 inches long. The containment structure would have been completely breached within two more months. Prior to this discovery, maintenance personnel regularly found rust particles "mysteriously clogging" air-conditioning and water filters. The clogging was severe enough that maintenance personnel were changing the air filters every two days for two years, whereas the industry norm was to change the filters once a month.[13] The rust accumulation was a weak signal of plantwide problems that might have been detected sooner had information about industrywide experience been disseminated more thoroughly, had local personnel compared this experience with filter replacement in other parts of the facility, had the purchasing department questioned the large orders for filter replacements, or simply if people had started asking around about whether replacement every forty-eight hours seemed out of line.

Preoccupation with failure is not confined to nuclear power generation. Other organizations tend to make strong responses to weak signals in the interest of reliable functioning. For example, a senior executive at an East Coast power company told us about an unconventional indicator that had proved diagnostic of larger system issues. When the incidence of bee stings goes up for electrical linemen working in the field, it's a sign that they are reaching into places without looking, and that means they may be getting sloppy when they handle active power lines. A second example, this one from the world of wildland firefighting, was captured in a remark by Mark Linane, a seasoned crew foreman. "The pucker factor goes up when you get out of camp late." If firefighters leave camp late to hike to a fire, by the time they get there, the temperature is higher, the grass is drier, the winds are stronger, and the fire is more active than people had anticipated. Firefighting becomes riskier.

Behind the principle of preoccupation with failure is the basic idea that "even with wide safety margins and detailed operating procedures, missteps, missing resources, miscommunications, or mistakes have to be found and put right before they can turn into a tragic flaw."[14] In HROs, the big issue is how long a problem lasts. "The longer problematic conditions persist, the less predictable and controllable system interactions become."[15] The earlier you catch a discrepancy, the more options you have to deal with it. But the earlier you try to catch an error, the harder it is to spot it.

Detecting Failure

Detecting failure is not as straightforward as it looks. It can start with a feeling (for example, you have a feeling that something isn't right, but just how right or wrong is a tough call to make).[16] Detection can also start with a checklist that alerts you to situations where expectations and practices may be especially shaky:

- Recent changes in supervision
- Issues delegated without follow-up
- Lack of a questioning attitude

- Missed steps in a procedure
- People not on the same page
- Staff spread thin
- Distraction from schedule pressures[17]

Human factors psychologist James Reason provides a different kind of checklist to spot where unforeseen events will surface. Reason suggests that failures are most likely to occur at the human-system interface and says that to assess this, managers should ask three questions:

1. The "hands on" question: What activities involve the most direct human contact with the system and thus offer the greatest opportunity for human decisions or actions to have an immediate, direct, adverse effect upon the system?
2. The "criticality" question: What activities, if performed less than adequately, pose the greatest risks to the well-being of the system?
3. The "frequency" question: How often are these activities performed in the day-to-day operation of the system as a whole?[18]

Maintenance personnel seem well positioned to spot unexpected problems and improve organizational learning. Normally, maintenance workers encounter failures at earlier stages of development and have an increased awareness of vulnerabilities in the technology, sloppiness in the operations, gaps in the procedures, and dependencies among problems. But this wasn't the case at Davis-Besse. Why not?[19] Among the many reasons is the fact that rust accumulation was not a failure that people felt was significant; nor was missing this kind of accumulation seen as "a mistake we can't make." Furthermore, speaking up and sharing information were not encouraged, and the plant lacked a "safety culture" that would have encouraged practices that were consistent with the other four principles of high reliability.

Although maintenance personnel may not be central in all organizations, there are parallel positions or units in which early signs of failure are visible. For example, people who work with warranty returns, customer service, and tech support hotlines often come into contact with surprises that shed light on an organization's more basic weaknesses. HROs are clear about who in the organization makes observations that are equivalent to maintenance observations.

Failure detection can also start with a list of expectations. Before an event (such as reactor shutdown) occurs, write down what you think will happen. Be specific. Seal the list in an envelope, and set it aside. After the event is over, reread your list and assess where you were right and wrong. Be vigilant when one of your expectations isn't confirmed. That could be a signal of trouble, which is rendered all the more important because failures in interdependent systems tend to come in clusters.

Finally, you can detect failures by being candid about your own failures. Candor about failed expectations encourages others to be similarly candid, improves the quality of data available for learning, introduces corrections earlier when emerging problems are more manageable, and reaffirms the truth that we're all fallible and most dangerous when we think we aren't.

The ability to detect failures early in their history can be hindered by several features of organizing. For example, if a small failure is to be treated as a clue to the health of the system, people have to be aware of its wider relevance. This awareness is unlikely if the system exists in name only and people live their organizational lives in separate, small "silos." Silos are common in nuclear power plants. This creates tension, as Constance Perin explains:

> At Overton Station, a manager drew an image of overlapping circles to represent their work systems, and when I showed it to a senior engineer from another station whose organizational chart typically showed boxes of functions and positions connected by reporting lines, he fumed, "If boxes become circles, functional boundaries

would disappear and there would be chaos. The person inside a box has the job of talking across boxes. But he shouldn't get out of his box and join another. Each function has to specialize and should not overlap."[20]

Boxes lead to silos, and silos make it harder to see systemwide failures.

Reporting Failure

To detect a failure is one thing. To report it is another. Research shows that people need to feel safe to report incidents or they will ignore them or cover them up. Managerial practices such as encouraging people to ask questions and rewarding people who report errors or mistakes strengthen an organizationwide culture that values reporting. In the nuclear power industry, reporting is also encouraged because all employees recognize that complex nuclear technology can fail in ways that no one has imagined and that the technology is still capable of surprise.

The best HROs increase their knowledge base by encouraging and rewarding error reporting, even going so far as to reward those who have committed the errors. For example, industrial sociologist Ron Westrum describes the lesson conveyed when Wernher von Braun sent a bottle of champagne to an engineer who, when a Redstone missile went out of control, reported that he may have caused a short-circuit during prelaunch testing. Analysis revealed that this had indeed caused the accident, and his confession meant that expensive redesigns were unnecessary.[21]

Researchers Martin Landau and Donald Chisholm provide a similar example. A seaman on the nuclear carrier *Carl Vinson* reported the loss of a tool on the deck. All aircraft aloft were redirected to land bases until the tool was found, and the seaman was commended for his action—recognizing a potential danger—the next day at a formal ceremony.[22] Harvard Business School professor Amy Edmondson found that the highest-performing nursing units had higher detected rates of error for adverse drug events than lower-performing units. She interprets these results to mean not that more errors were committed in the high-performing units but that a climate of openness made people more willing to report and discuss errors, work toward correcting them, and learn more about the system in the process.[23] Subsequent research has refined Edmondson's finding by showing that when people do learn from open discussion of higher rates of error, error rates do decrease in the high-performing units.[24]

Is Failure as Bad as It Sounds?

Some people resist the phrase "preoccupation with failure" because it suggests that any unexpected event is the result of someone's failure and therefore has moral overtones. Any such suggestion seems to imply that someone is to blame for the failure, not that something can be learned from it. Before getting caught up in these associations, keep in mind that the dictionary defines reliability as "what one can count on not to fail while doing what is expected of it." Three questions arise here:

1. What do people count on?
2. What do people expect from the things they count on?
3. In what ways can the things people count on fail?

The answers to these three questions provide clues about *what* it is that could go wrong and *what* it is that you don't want to go wrong. The key word in all three questions is *what* one can count on, not *who*. A preoccupation with failure is a preoccupation with maintaining reliable performance. And reliable performance is a system issue (a "what"), not an individual issue (a "who"). Failures are connected. Small events that are the outcome of earlier, more distant conditions predispose subsequent events to deviate from the expected.

Failures that include misspecification, misestimation, and misunderstanding have histories that stretch back before their appearance in unexpected events. These histories give off small indications of discrepancies along the way, discrepancies that are easy to spot in hindsight but hard to see at the time. Thus to be preoccupied with failure is to be attuned to indications along the way that small discrepancies are enlarging.[25] It is this path involving *growth* of the unexpected that leads us to make a different set of assumptions than those associated with the well-known "Swiss cheese model" used to explain the occurrence of industrial and organizational crises and accidents.[26] That model portrays chains of events as holes in separate slices of Swiss cheese that line up in such a way that defenses are breached and an accident occurs. Our interest, and that of HROs, is in the process of the slices lining up. Each moment where one hole aligns with another represents a failed expectation. And each failed expectation is also an opportunity to stop the progression toward a brutal audit.

Worries about failure are functional simply because there are limits to foresight. That is why people in HROs have been described as skeptical, wary, suspicious of quiet periods. This lingering wariness is especially mindful when people have experienced success. New York University Business School professors Bill Starbuck (emeritus) and Frances Milliken spotted several of these liabilities when they reanalyzed the January 28, 1986, *Challenger* disaster that killed seven astronauts. "Success breeds confidence and fantasy. When an organization succeeds, its managers usually attribute success to themselves or at least to their organization, rather than to luck. The organization's members grow more confident of their own abilities, of their manager's skills, and of their organization's existing programs and procedures. They trust the procedures to keep them apprised of developing problems, in the belief that these procedures focus on the most important events and ignore the least significant ones."[27]

Success narrows perceptions, changes attitudes, reinforces a single way of doing business, breeds overconfidence in the adequacy of current practices, and reduces acceptance of opposing points of view. The problem is that if people assume that success demonstrates competence, they are more likely to drift into complacency, inattention, and predictable routines. What they don't realize is that complacency also increases the likelihood that unexpected events will go undetected longer and accumulate into bigger problems. The best antidote to this trap is dwelling on failures as much as on success. And success is such a heady feeling that it takes a *preoccupation* with failure to keep it in awareness.

To summarize, HROs are preoccupied with failure in two ways. First, they work hard to detect small emerging failures because these may be a clue to additional failures elsewhere in the system. Second, HROs work hard to anticipate and specify significant mistakes that they don't want to make. Ongoing attention to these potentially significant failures is built into their practices. HROs are therefore preoccupied with events that deviate from what they expected, especially deviations that foreshadow strategically significant failures. In both cases, the preoccupation is warranted because the causal chains that produce failures can wind deep into the organization and be hard to spot. It takes more than mere attentiveness to stay on top of this complexity. That's why preoccupation is a hallmark of HROs.

Principle 2: Reluctance to Simplify

A strong message of Chapter Two was that expectations simplify the world and steer observers away from the very disconfirming evidence that foreshadows unexpected problems. And mindfulness, with its insistence on closer attention to context, categories, and expectations was proposed as a way to counteract these simplifications. With closer attention to context comes more differentiation of worldviews and mind-sets. And with more differentiation comes a richer and more varied picture of potential consequences, which in turn suggests a richer and more varied set of precautions and early warning signs. HROs are just as preoccupied with complicating their simplifications as they are with probing their failures. But just as it's hard to dwell on your failures rather than your successes, it's hard to complicate your categories rather than lump them into actionable simplicities such as "make or buy," "friend or enemy," "profit or loss." The difficulties notwithstanding, people in HROs wage a relentless attack on simplifications.

"Relentless attack" may sound a bit melodramatic. But just such an approach is necessary if people want to detect small failures that foreshadow larger problems. Organizations survive by means of their simplifications. As organizational theorist Hari Tsoukas puts it, the essence of organizing is simplification. To say that any activity is "organized" implies that "types of behavior in types of situations are connected to types of actors. . . . An organized activity provides actors with a given set of cognitive categories and a typology of action options. . . . [Thus] organizing implies generalizing; the subsumption of heterogeneous particulars under generic categories. In that sense, formal organization necessarily involves abstraction."[28] Early warning signs lie buried in those heterogeneous details. And those signs go undetected when details are lumped into generic categories. That's why HROs simplify slowly, reluctantly, mindfully.

The Hazards of Labels

In Chapter Two, we mentioned that NASA distinguishes between events that are "in-family" and those that are "out-of-family." An in-family event is "a reportable problem that was previously experienced, analyzed, and understood."[29] The point made then was that whatever words you use when you report a problem determine meaning, action, and consequences. We see this happen in nuclear power plants when they distinguish between "minor work" and "major work." "In a year filled with, say, 10,000 work orders, 'minor' and 'major' are welcome categories announcing priorities and demarcating responsibilities. But in such 'language habits of the group,' there is likely to be little difference between naming categories and living up to them."[30] People "live up" to the label "minor work" when they postpone it until the last day of the workweek, with connotations of low significance and low priority. Believing is seeing. And believing that the work is "minor" leads people to see those aspects that confirm this expectation. What they miss are small departures that might have been detected had the seeing been driven by more refined, more consequential labels.

The classic example of living up to categories is the word *empty*. Linguist Benjamin Whorf is credited with the discovery that meanings, not just physical conditions, were often responsible for fires and explosions. His example involved drums of gasoline. A drum filled with gasoline is explosive and must be handled with great care. An "empty" gasoline drum implies that it has nothing in it and can therefore be treated more casually (for example, smoking a cigarette near the drum doesn't sound like it would be a problem). However, empty gasoline drums are actually more dangerous than full drums because the empty drum is filled with vapor, which is more explosive than gasoline. Using the word *empty* to describe the drum masks that fact. As obvious as Whorf's example is, the very situation he described killed 110 people when ValuJet Flight 592 caught fire and crashed in Florida in May 1996. The plane caught fire when "empty" oxygen generators that were carried in the hold ignited because they still held volatile components.[31]

The Hazards of Shared Labels

If you want to resist simplification, you can't simply avoid categories. That's impossible. But what you can do is suggested by two examples from nuclear power generation. Here's a simple example: people who work in the power plant don't trust the simplifications found in drawings and blueprints.[32] If they have an assignment to shut down something, such as the air supply in a nonoperating unit, they won't do so until they actually walk down the whole system, looking for valves, added piping, or reroutes that have been made since the drawings were completed. Those recent add-ons that are missing from the drawings are potential sources of serious surprises.

Here's a more complex example: people who work with nuclear power use many of the same means to resist simplification that we saw in flight operations on aircraft carriers. The best example of this similarity is the reliance on constant interaction. Commenting on activity at Diablo Canyon, researcher Paul Schulman noted:

> When faced with failure, members of the plant's departments can be readily observed in meetings, where they question the interpretation of other departments and add their own perspective on what's at risk in a proposed course of action. In effect, interacting with one another, employees generate hypotheses about what is going on, what can be done, and what the long-term, system-wide consequences of proposed actions might be. This is their way of coping with the potential for surprise within the enormously complex technology they are trying to control.[33]

It's not just the interaction itself that reduces simplification. It's the fact that the interaction is among people who have *diverse expectations*. Teams composed of at least some individuals with different expertise are better able to grasp variations in their environments and to see specific changes that need to be made. They also are better at coping—especially when they think they have the capability to act on what they see. Moreover generalist teams—teams that include at least some individuals who have had a broad range of experiences—are better at recombining existing knowledge, skills, and abilities into novel combinations.[34] Because action and cognition are linked, as a team increases its capabilities for action, it enhances the group's capabilities to register and handle complexity. This diversity enables people to see different things when they view the "same" event. We see this dynamic operating in many different places. Almost all the oversight groups at Diablo Canyon (for example, the equipment modification subgroup, regulatory nonconformance subgroup, and incident investigation subgroup) have members from multiple units.[35] Since each unit has a different set of vested interests and a different set of expectations, its representatives see different things.

But simply seeing different things in the same event still leaves a big problem. This problem involves what social psychologists

Reuben Baron and Stephen Misovich call the "shareability constraint."[36] While this may sound like one more unintelligible phrase, it is a great choice of wording. They argue that when we as individuals make sense of something like an unexpected event, we do so through active exploration. Active exploration does *not* immediately require that we name something. Thus we start with knowledge by direct acquaintance. But if we start to name what we have seen, the names we use, rather than the impressions we sensed, take over. As names take over, we begin to develop knowledge by description rather than by acquaintance. When this shift occurs, we go beyond the information we started with and lump those initial perceptions into types, categories, and stereotypes.

The importance of this shift for reliable organizing is that if you want to share your initial impressions and talk about them, those impressions have to take on a particular form. As social complexity increases, we shift from knowing that is based on direct acquaintance to knowing that is based on linguistic categories. We make this shift in the interest of coordination. But these gains in coordination lose many of the distinctive details that we picked up earlier by direct perception. When we concentrate on coordination, we tend to remember the *name* of the thing rather than the qualities that we observed and felt. If we lose those qualities in some general name, we also risk losing early warnings of the unexpected.

As if a reluctance to simplify were not hard enough, now we add the suggestion that people should also be reluctant to coordinate. Recall what our priorities are. At the most basic level, we want to design organizations that can manage the unexpected. This means that designs need to help people detect the unexpected as early as possible. And early detection depends on the names we impose on what we experience. As organizational theorist Gerardo Patriotta explains, our universe is preinterpreted. We see in the world what our stock of interpretations "allows" us to see. The variety in these interpretations determines how much variation we can sense.[37]

In social relationships and interactions, generic categories draw our attention away from details. And when we lose details, we lose early warning signs. Details get lost in generics. And they get lost in vagueness. We mask deviations when we use vague verbs such as *impact*, *affect*, and *determine*; vague adjectives such as *slow*, *sufficient*, and *periodic*; and vague phrases such as *as soon as*, *if required*, and *when directed*.[38] When we say more clearly what we often keep vague for political reasons, we become more alert to potential brutal audits that lurk farther downstream.

Carrying Categories More Lightly

Although categories are unavoidable, we can carry them more lightly. If you want to carry a category more lightly, you need both to believe and to doubt it. If you can do that, you are that much closer to wise action.[39] You can also carry your categories more lightly if you differentiate them into subcategories, treat them as a blind spot as well as a source of illumination, question the assumptions that support them, and examine closely examples that fit the category imperfectly to see what *new* category they suggest. All of these variations accept the reality that events are preinterpreted. Knowing that those preinterpretations simplify details that may signify trouble, HROs impose them warily. As a result, details are preserved because simplifications occur more slowly, varied forms of simplification are imposed, and needs for simplification themselves are reduced.

Principle 3: Sensitivity to Operations

Here's what sensitivity to operations looks like in a nuclear power plant. The plant manager at Diablo Canyon described control room operators as people who

> have a bubble, a 3-D picture. They look at the control room and see the plant. If a needle goes up it should then come down. If not something's wrong. They have a mental picture in which once you learn

the board you stop seeing it. You operate the plant as though it was an animal. The best operator is the guy who worked at the plant before it went on line. He crawled through the plant.[40]

During outages at Diablo Canyon, meetings for updates and briefings are held throughout the day. These interdisciplinary and interdepartmental meetings are important for two reasons. First, they increase the credibility and trust needed among departments to coordinate complex tasks. Meetings help prevent turf wars that could threaten operations at the plant. Second, constant interaction deepens people's understanding of the interdependent workings of the complex system itself. This helps people cope more effectively with unexpected surprises.[41] Professor Mathilde Bourrier found dense interaction in the handling of planned outages in the best nuclear power plants.[42] Top management people were available throughout the outage, so any problem could receive attention rapidly from all levels of the organization. This structure works largely because everyone also remains informed of what is happening and how the intervention is progressing.

The Meaning of Sensitivity to Operations

When we say HROs are sensitive to operations, we mean that they are responsive to the messy reality inside most systems. To be sensitive to operations is to monitor "expectable interactions with a complicated [and] often opaque system" and to respond promptly to those unexpected.[43] That may sound a lot like the first two principles of reliable functioning that involve failure and simplification, but it's not. Preoccupation with failure is about detecting small discrepancies anywhere. Reluctance to simplify is about the concepts people have at hand to do the detecting. And sensitivity to operations is about the work itself, about seeing what we are *actually* doing regardless of what we were supposed to do based on intentions, designs, and plans. Admiral Hyman Rickover, leader of the team that developed a submarine nuclear reactor in the late 1940s, was sensitive to operations when he claimed that too much attention was being paid to research and development and too little attention to "the daily drudgery of seeing that every aspect . . . is in fact properly handled every day by each of the organizations involved."[44] Medical personnel were sensitive to operations when they noticed that an unusually high number of needle stick injuries among cleaning personnel may have occurred because the trash can was located right under the syringe bucket. They moved the trash can. The needle sticks stopped.

What is distinctive about the better HROs is that when they put the principle of sensitivity to operations into practice, they perform activities that accept the ambiguities of intentions and work hard to give undivided attention to small deviations and interruptions in operations.

Threats to Sensitivity to Operations

The primary threat to operations in nuclear plants is the engineering culture, which places a higher value on knowledge that is quantitative, measurable, hard, objective, and formal and a lower value on the more experiential knowledge needed by operators to fulfill the engineers' intentions. Doubt, discovery, and on-the-spot interpretation are hallmarks of sensitivity. But in a nuclear culture that values experience-distant, context-free formalization built on models and simulations, operators who make experience-based, context-bound interventions tend to be regarded as less rational. Yet it is those very same "less rational" practices that make the engineering intentions work.

HROs refuse to draw a hard line between knowledge that is quantitative and knowledge that is qualitative. Neither stands higher than the other in the HRO value hierarchy. If you want to manage unexpected events, you need to put a premium on the detection of small failures, differentiation of categories, and watchfulness for moment-to-moment changes in condition. You also need to appreciate that relationships and continuous conversation are essential to handling risks that designs have not anticipated. The benefits of being sensitive to operations also show up in contexts other than HROs. As Stanford University professor Kathleen Eisenhardt found, the best performers in the microcomputer industry pay close attention to real-time information through frequent operations meetings, widely disseminated operational measures of performance, and nearly continuous face-to-face interaction.[45]

A second threat to sustained sensitivity is the tendency of routines to become mindless. The words *mindless* and *routine* are not synonyms, and the better HROs are clear about the difference. *Mindless* acts are automatic, *routine* ones merely customary. If you assume that *routine* refers to an automatic activity, as in the phrase "It's a routine job," you run the risk that people will forget to ask the question "What if . . . ?" "If you have a cramped schedule of normal jobs, you tend to think of 'what ifs' as a waste of time."[46] For example, maintenance people who work on valves every day may do so mindlessly, or they can work more mindfully and say, essentially, I have this valve to work on. "What system is it on, and what's the worst thing that can happen?"[47] When operators execute operations mindfully, they tend to rework the routine to fit changed conditions and to update the routine when there is new learning. These small adjustments are the bane of a command-and-control system. But those same adjustments keep the system going even as they sustain the illusion that it is commands and rule compliance, not continuing adjustments, that keep it going.

A final threat to operations is an overestimation of their soundness. This happens most often when people learn the wrong lessons from close calls. Close calls sharpen the meaning of failure in relation to success. The most effective HROs regard close calls—for example, a near collision in aviation—as a kind of failure that reveals potential danger. In contrast, less effective HROs do just the opposite: they look at a near miss and interpret it as evidence of safety and their ability to avoid disaster. When people see a near miss as success, this reinforces their beliefs that current operations are sufficient to forestall unintended consequences. The *Challenger* disaster, mentioned earlier in this chapter, is a good illustration. NASA repeatedly interpreted grease and burn marks behind the O-rings as within the limits of acceptable risk because the shuttles continued to complete their missions. As the burns marks became larger and more severe, the severity kept being reinterpreted as safety in the guise of danger rather than danger in the guise of safety. The problem was that the limits of acceptable risk kept getting larger. As people began to treat these warning signals as normal, the system became more vulnerable. These signals had a clear direction that indicated they were not randomly distributed. Insensitivity to operations missed this pattern.

HROs worry about the blind spots that are associated with safe interpretations of a near miss. The principle of sensitivity to operations is a guideline that can offset some of this blindness if it is translated into practices that focus on actual work rather than intentions, define actual work by its relationships rather than its parts, and treat routine work as anything but automatic.

Acting with Anticipation: A Summary

Reliability-enhancing organizations enact a number of processes to improve their capabilities to anticipate and become aware of the unexpected earlier so that people can act before problems become severe. These practices are based on three principles, involving failure, simplification, and operations. When these principles are expressed in local practices, members do such things as these:

- They persuade all their members to be chronically concerned about the unexpected and sensitive to the fact that in the face of the potential for surprise, any decision or action may be subject to faulty assumptions or errors in analysis.
- They work to create a climate where people feel safe to question assumptions and to report problems or failures candidly.

- They help people expand the number of undesired consequences they envision so that they can expand the number of precautions they will take.

- They encourage organizational members to view close calls as a kind of failure that reveals potential danger, rather than as evidence of success and the ability to avoid disaster.

- They create a climate where people are wary of success, suspicious of quiet periods, and concerned about stability, routinization, and lack of challenge and variety that can predispose their organization to relax vigilance and sink into complacency that can lead to carelessness and error.

- They counteract tendencies to simplify assumptions, expectations, and analyses through practices such as adversarial reviews, selection of employees with nontypical prior experience, frequent job rotation, and retraining.

- They work to create a climate that encourages variety in people's analyses of the organization's technology and production processes and establish practices that allow those perspectives to be heard and to surface information not held in common. They also train people to manage these differences.

- They pay serious attention to operations, the front line, and imperfections in these features. They set in place operating practices that help people develop a collective map of operations at any given moment.

Chapter Summary

Anticipation, which involves tracking the development of unexpected events, is done more mindfully when practices are preoccupied with failure, reluctant to simplify details, and sensitive to operations. The first principle involving failure is based on the assumption that gradual, interconnected development of unexpected events sends weak signals of this development along the way. A preoccupation with failure catches these signals earlier, when it is easier to correct them and learn from them. It is emphasized that success also has liabilities and may produce failures such as overconfidence, reduced safety margins, and elimination of redundancies. The second principle involving simplification is based on the assumption that the diagnostic value of weak signals is lost when those details are lumped into crude, general categories. Categories may improve coordination, but they harm detection of events not seen before. The third principle involving operations is based on the assumption that plans and designs reflect intentions that are rational but context-free and can be implemented only if context-sensitive experiential rationality is applied to them. Sensitivity to operations takes the form of interpretive practices that doubt the applicability of intentions and then discover ways to transform the intentions into meaningful actions in a specific context.

Principles of anticipation focus on the prevention of disruptive unexpected events. But unexpected events sometimes continue to develop despite efforts to spot early failures, preserve details, and monitor operations. When this happens, mindful attention shifts to practices of containment. Those practices are guided by two principles—commitment to resilience and deference to expertise—which are the focus of Chapter Four.

4

Principles of Containment

By definition, errors, surprises, and the unexpected are difficult to anticipate. As you saw in Chapter Three, HROs deal with this difficulty by trying to improve their ability to anticipate. They invest resources in such activities as developing contingency plans, imagining a greater range of worst-case scenarios, and detecting hazards early in their development. The intention in all of these efforts is to prevent small unexpected outcomes from worsening.

But HROs are mindful of the limitations of foresight and anticipation. Sometimes precautions fail, and unexpected events begin to escalate into a crisis. Then what? HROs of all kinds seem to be guided by at least two principles—commitment to building resilience and deference to expertise—that enable them to contain and bounce back from problems mindfully. Before we delve into these principles, we should say more about the shift from anticipation to containment.

Containment differs from anticipation in that it aims to prevent unwanted outcomes *after* an unexpected event has occurred rather than to prevent the unexpected event itself.[1] Unexpected events begin to unfold before they are noticed. This means that organizational reliability depends on how well prepared the organization is to be mindfully *reactive*. The importance of *reacting* mindfully and swiftly is one reason we opened this book with the examples of good and bad practice in firefighting.

Three Problems Posed
by Anticipation and Planning

Organizations create plans to prepare for the inevitable, preempt the undesirable, and control the controllable. Rational as all this may sound, planning has its shortcomings. Because planners plan in stable, predictable contexts, they are lulled into thinking that the world will unfold in the expected manner, a lapse that Henry Mintzberg calls "the fallacy of predetermination."[2] When people are in thrall of predetermination, there is simply no place for unexpected events that fall outside the realm of planning.

Plans, in short, can do just the opposite of what is intended, creating mindlessness instead of mindful anticipation of the unexpected. They do so in at least three ways. First, since plans are built from assumptions and beliefs about the world, they embody expectations. Strong expectations influence what people see, what they choose to take for granted, what they choose to ignore, and the length of time it takes to recognize small problems that are growing. When people impose their expectations on ambiguous stimuli, they typically fill in the gaps, read between the lines, and complete the picture as best they can. Typically, this means that they complete the picture in ways that confirm what they expected to see. Slight deviations from the normal course of events are smoothed over and quickly lose their salience. It is only after a space shuttle explodes or illicit trading is exposed or vehicle tires come apart that people see a clear and ominous pattern in the weak signals they had previously dismissed.

By design, then, plans influence perception and reduce the number of things people notice. This occurs because people encode the world largely into the categories activated by the plan. Anything that is deemed "irrelevant" to the plan gets only cursory attention. And yet it is these very irrelevancies that are the seedbed of the unexpected events that make for unreliable functioning.

The second problem is that plans can undercut organizational functioning because they specify contingent actions that are designed to cope with the future. The problem is, these contingent actions are doubly blind. They are blind because they restrict attention to what we expect. And they are blind because they limit our present view of our capabilities to those we now have. When we plan contingent actions, we tend not to imagine how we might recombine the actions in our current repertoire to deal with the unexpected. In other words, contingency plans preclude improvisation.

The third problem is that plans presume that consistent high-quality outcomes will be produced time after time if people repeat patterns of activity that have worked in the past. The problem with this logic is that routines can't handle novel events. A perfect example of how people lose flexibility in the face of extensive rules and procedures is researcher Larry Hirschhorn's description of the problems maintenance workers had when they needed to lift wires to complete an assigned task in a nuclear plant but could find no procedure for doing so. Mechanics lifted the wire to complete their work. But this created a problem for the technicians assigned to test the motor before it was put back online because "the testing procedures did not cover the situation in which maintenance workers lifted the wires!"[3] The point is that you cannot write procedures to anticipate all the situations and conditions that shape people's work. If unexpected events are to be managed, this means that people have to change what they do but not their way of sensing that something needs to be done. And this is precisely the point that the most effective HROs seem to have grasped. They understand that reliable outcomes require the capabilities to *sense* the unexpected in a *stable* manner and yet *deal with* the unexpected in a *variable* manner. This variation in coping processes is what we have in mind in the following discussion of principles of containment.

HROs are able to implement this complex reaction because of their stable mindful infrastructure. For example, Paul Schulman observed that operators at the Diablo Canyon nuclear power plant continually altered their actions and interactions to deal with the unexpected, but they did *not* alter their mindful processes of

understanding, evidence collection, detection, evaluation, and re-
vising.[4] These mindful processes became the stable routines that
triggered the variable activities that managed the unexpected. Most
organizations don't act this way. Under the influences of routines
and expectations, they tend to keep their activities constant and
vary their processes of mindfulness, precisely the opposite of what
HROs do.

Principle 4: Commitment to Resilience

Nowhere in this book will you find any mention of perfection, zero
errors, flawless performance, or infallible humans. That's because
"human fallibility is like gravity, weather, and terrain, just another
foreseeable hazard."[5] If errors are inevitable, managers should be just
as concerned with cures as they now are with prevention. To be resilient is to be mindful about errors *that have already occurred* and to
correct them before they worsen and cause more serious harm. If
you take a close look at the phrase "managing the unexpected," you
will notice that the word *unexpected* refers to something that has already happened. When you manage the unexpected, you're always
playing catch-up. You face something that has happened that you
did not anticipate.

Think about the problems of anticipating a disease outbreak
such as West Nile virus or the hantavirus, both of which involved
a pattern never seen before.[6] Robin Henig states that "there is no
good way to anticipate the next disease outbreak short of waiting
for a few people to get sick."[7] What is the next AIDS? You can't do
much until the first wave of human infection occurs. If you find a
new virus, you don't know whether it is significant or not until a
human episode occurs. The trouble is that by the time you do establish that it is significant, the virus has already settled in. Edwin
Kilbourne, a virologist at the Mount Sinai School of Medicine, describes the reactive quality of diagnosis: "I think in a sense we have
to be prepared to do what the Centers for Disease Control does so
very well, and that is *put out fire*. . . . It's not intellectually very sat-

isfying to wait to react to a situation, but I think there's only so much preliminary planning you can do. I think the preliminary planning has to focus on what you do when the emergency happens: Is your fire company well drilled? Are they ready to act, or are they sitting around the station house for months."[8]

Notice that in the reactive world of the unexpected, the ability to make sense out of an emerging pattern is just as important as anticipation and planning. And the ability to cope with the unexpected requires a different mind-set than to anticipate its occurrence. The mind-set for anticipation is one that favors precise identification of possible difficulties so that specific remedies can be designed or recalled. A commitment to resilience is quite different.

The Nature of Resilience

Aaron Wildavsky describes the nature of a commitment to resilience: "The mode of resilience is based on the assumption that unexpected trouble is ubiquitous and unpredictable; and thus accurate advance information on how to get out of it is in short supply. To learn from error (as opposed to avoiding error altogether) and to implement that learning through fast negative feedback, which dampens oscillations, are at the forefront of operating resiliently."[9] Resilient people think mitigation rather than anticipation. They are attentive to expanding general knowledge, technical facility, and command over resources that relieve, lighten, moderate, reduce, and decrease surprises.[10]

Formally, resilience is the "capability of a system to maintain its function and structure in the face of internal and external changes and to degrade gracefully when it must."[11] Resilience occurs when the system continues to operate despite failures in some of its parts. For example, an electric toothbrush degrades gracefully because it can still be used as a toothbrush even if the motor doesn't work. Resilient organizations or systems either are able to continue operations or to quickly recover their stability during or after a mishap or in the presence of continuous significant stresses.[12] HROs try to degrade gracefully rather than suffer a total breakdown in which normal functioning stops and the return is gradual.[13]

Resilience is a form of control. "A system is in control if it is able to minimize or eliminate unwanted variability, either in its own performance, in the environment, or in both. . . . The fundamental characteristic of a resilient organization is that it does not lose control of what it does but is able to continue and rebound."[14]

Here's an example of resilience from FedEx.[15] The FedEx Global Operations Control Unit manages what the company calls the "sweep network." Every evening, twenty to twenty-five aircraft in the domestic system start their flights toward Memphis only 60 percent loaded. The remaining space is left empty; this allows aircraft to be diverted on their way to Memphis in order to recover "at risk" cargo. "At risk" cargo is product that was unanticipated (for example, Dell ships more pallets of computers than anticipated). A portion of FedEx's mission statement supplies the premises for the company's commitment to resilience. A portion of the statement reads as follows:

> Global Operations Control (GOC) seeks to ensure that service commitments are met and that minimum disruption occurs due to mechanical problems, weather conditions, operating/regulatory requirements, and volume fluctuations. As caretakers of the line haul system, Global Operations Control has considerable opportunity to impact service to the customer directly. The goal of GOC is to move 100% of the packages on time. GOC is prepared to respond to any exception that arises. The use of foresight, creativity, conservative decisions, and above all, common sense in the management of the line haul system is vital to improve the level of reliability for the customer.

That could well be the credo for any high reliability system. FedEx does not attempt to recover "at risk" cargo if it puts more customers at risk than are already at risk. The rule of thumb for deciding whether or not a sweep will work is to calculate the time needed to fly the divert route and allow thirty minutes for ground time. If that allows the aircraft to arrive in Memphis by 1:30 A.M., do it. If it doesn't, find another sweep aircraft. And if that can't be done, don't take down the system by bending the hard deadline of 1:30 A.M.

What we see in the case of FedEx is that the company *anticipates* that surprises of some sort will occur every night. FedEx tries to *contain* these surprises by using practices that enact resilience. Aircraft that are 40 percent empty provide space for the system to stretch without collapsing. The thirty minutes allotted for ground time compel the stretched system to bounce back to its original timeline of arrival in Memphis by 1:30. What we also see in the FedEx example is that resilient people think about mitigation as well as anticipation. The FedEx system shows elasticity as well as the capability to maintain most of its original form. People are attentive to knowledge and resources that reduce surprises. The mind-set is one of cure rather than prevention. People are willing to begin treating an anomaly even before they have made a full diagnosis. They do so in the belief that their action will enable them to gain experience and a clearer picture of what they are treating. Unlike anticipation, which encourages people to think and then act, resilience encourages people to act while thinking or to act in order to think more clearly.

Components of Resilience

Resilience involves three abilities: (1) the ability to absorb strain and preserve functioning despite the presence of adversity (both internal adversity, such as rapid change, lousy leadership, and performance and production pressures, and external adversity, such as increasing competition and demands from stakeholders); (2) an ability to recover or bounce back from untoward events—as the system becomes better able to absorb a surprise and stretch rather than collapse, the "brutality" of an audit decreases; and (3) an ability to learn and grow from previous episodes of resilient action.

What happens during the recovery from a stretch can be crucial for the subsequent fate of the system. When a system absorbs the unexpected and bounces back, what does it bounce back to? It can return to its original position. But it can also return to an area reasonably close to its original position or it can be transformed to a different position and begin to become a different entity. The important question for reliable performance and managing the unexpected is, what happens to the original capability for flexibility and resilience when a perturbed system settles back down? Is that capability decreased, increased, or the same? This question matters because systems often respond to a disturbance with new rules and new prohibitions designed to prevent the same disruption from happening in the future. This response *reduces* flexibility to deal with subsequent unpredictable changes.[16] But reduction of flexibility is not inevitable. HROs tend to respond to disturbance with new learning (both content and process) and a larger experience base, both of which preserve flexibility. Every unexpected event has some resemblance to previous events and some novelty relative to previous events. Resilient action registers this mixed character of the unexpected by bouncing back to the area of the original position rather than to the precise point where it was prior to the disturbance. The resilient system bears the marks of its dealings with the unexpected not in the form of more elaborate defenses but in the form of more elaborate response capabilities.[17]

Patterns of Resilience

HROs overcome error when interdependent people with varied experience apply a richer set of resources to a disturbance at great speed and under the guidance of swift negative feedback. This is fast realtime learning that allows people to cope with an unfolding surprise in diverse ways that are unspecified in advance. In a curious inversion of common managerial images, managers in HROs take pride in the fact that they spend their time putting out fires, whereas most managers lament the time they devote to putting out fires. Managers in HROs regard successful firefighting as evidence that they are resilient and able to contain the unexpected. Most managers in business regard successful firefighting as evidence that they are distracted by daily nuisances and unable to do their "real work" of strategizing, planning, and anticipating.

HROs committed to resilience assume that they will be surprised, so they concentrate on developing general resources to cope with and respond to change swiftly. This means that they work to develop knowledge, capability for swift feedback, faster learning, speed and accuracy of communication, experiential variety, skill at recombination of existing response repertoires, and comfort with improvisation. At Diablo Canyon, for example, a commitment to resilience is evident in a culture that encourages the widespread conviction among all its members that formal procedures are fallible. The mind-set is, since we have not experienced all the ways in which things can fail, we must be continually wary.[18] A commitment to resilience is evident in training that is designed (1) to build people's skill in mentally simulating plant operations, how they can unravel, and how they might be corrected and (2) to develop their capabilities to cope with a disturbance and learn from their experience. A commitment to resilience is evident in management practices and organizational norms that encourage *conceptual slack*. Conceptual slack refers to a divergence in organizational members' analytical perspectives about the organization's technology or production processes, a willingness to question what is happening rather than feign understanding, and greater usage of respectful interaction to accelerate and enrich the exchange of information.[19]

A commitment to resilience is difficult to sustain because you have to keep learning without knowing in advance just what you will be learning or how it will be applied. Your challenge is to avoid adjusting to surprises in ways that reduce adaptability. Adjusting to unexpected situations can undermine adaptability, but it won't if you're committed to resilience.

Principle 5: Deference to Expertise

To be mindful in the face of unexpected operating contingencies, HROs have created a set of operating dynamics that are grounded in a deference to expertise. This process is less obvious than it sounds.

HROs don't simply assign the problem to an expert and then move on. Hierarchical patterns of authority exist in HROs, as they do in most traditional organizations. During routine operations, members of typical organizations demonstrate deference to the powerful, the coercive, and the senior, forgetting that higher-ups may have had the same experience over and over, were never on the shop floor, were not around when the plant was constructed, or may have acquired their position through politics. Since people in higher positions often get nothing but filtered good news, those senior people continue to believe that things are going well. This filtering can work against managing the unexpected. As an unexpected event begins to materialize, someone somewhere sees early warning signs. But the first to know tend to be lower in rank, invisible, reluctant to speak up, and may not even realize that what they are seeing is important. What HROs have mastered is the ability to alter these typical patterns of deference as the tempo of operations increases and unexpected problems arise.

Karlene Roberts, Susanne Stout, and Jennifer Halpern identified what has come to be perhaps the most cited property of HROs: migrating decisions, both up and down. The idea of migration, first developed to make sense of flight operations on carriers, is described this way:

> Decisions are pushed down to the lowest levels in the carriers as a result of the need for quick decision making. Men who can immediately sense the potential problem can indeed make a quick decision to alleviate the problem or effectively decouple some of the technology, reducing the consequences of errors in decision making. . . . Decisions migrate around these organizations in search of a person who has specific knowledge of the event.[20]

Expertise is not necessarily matched with hierarchical position, so organizations that live or die by their hierarchy are seldom in a position to know all they can about a problem.

Failures of Deference and the *Columbia* Space Disaster

The complications that can occur when people do not defer to expertise are illustrated by the events surrounding NASA's management of the ill-fated mission STS-107 involving the *Columbia* space shuttle.[21] In the early stage of the flight, launched on January 16, 2003, three different groups were bothered by a puff of smoke that was barely visible on blurred photos taken eighty-two seconds into the flight. Each group requested clearer images of possible damage that had been inflicted on the shuttle. Mission manager Linda Ham considered the requests and asked *who* was requesting the additional images of Columbia, rather than *what* the merits of the request were.[22] At that time, rank mattered at NASA, and rank and expertise did not necessarily coincide.

The continuing debate in STS-107 over whether or not to secure more images was noteworthy for the ways in which expertise was neglected. For example, "No individuals in the STS-107 operational chain of command had the security clearance necessary to know about national imaging capabilities. . . . Members of the Mission Management team were making critical decisions about imagery capabilities based on little or no knowledge."[23] Managers thought, for example, that the orbiter would have to make a time-consuming change from its scheduled path to move it over Hawaii, where a new image of the damaged area could be made. What no one knew was that Hawaii was not the only facility that was available.[24] No one knew, no one asked, and no one listened.

The Columbia Accident Investigation Board fingered the issue of a lack of deference to expertise as a key contributor to the *Columbia* accident. "NASA's culture of bureaucratic accountability emphasized chain of command, procedure, following the rules, and going by the book. While rules and procedures were essential for coordination, they had an unintended negative effect. Allegiance to hierarchy and procedure had replaced deference to NASA engineers' technical expertise."[25]

When NASA did defer to expertise during the flight of STS-107, it did so in a manner that kept it from learning what it wanted to know. Within hours of the launch, people identified the site of the debris strike as the thermal protection system,[26] which meant that it could be a problem with tiles or the reinforced carbon-carbon (RCC) covering of the wing. These two sites of possible damage have quite different properties. The problem was labeled a tile problem, due in part to the fact that management listened mainly to experts who agreed with top management's expectation (and hope) that the damage to *Columbia* was minimal. Calvin Schomburg, "an engineer with close connections to Shuttle management,"[27] was regarded by managers as an expert on the thermal protection system even though he was not an expert on RCC (Don Curry was the resident RCC expert).[28] "Because neither Schomburg nor Shuttle management rigorously differentiated between tiles and RCC panels, the bounds of Schomburg's expertise were never properly qualified or questioned."[29]

Thus a tile expert told managers during frequent consultations that the damage was only a maintenance-level concern and that on-orbit imaging of potential wing damage was not necessary. "Mission management welcomed this opinion and sought no others. This constant reinforcement of managers' pre-existing beliefs added another block to the wall between decision makers and concerned engineers."[30] Earlier in the report, we find this additional comment: "As what the [Investigation] Board calls an 'informal chain of command' began to shape STS-107's outcome, location in the structure empowered some to speak and silenced others. For example, a Thermal Protection System tile expert, who was a member of the Debris Assessment Team but had an office in the more prestigious Shuttle Program, used his personal network to shape the Mission Management Team view and snuff out dissent."[31]

Andrew Hopkins, commenting on *Columbia*, noted that decisions "were not made by the engineers best equipped to make those decisions but by senior NASA officials who were protected by NASA's bureaucratic structure from the debates about the wisdom of the proposed actions."[32] A culture that is less mindful and more deferential to hierarchy is less informed by frontline experience and expertise and is more informed by inputs that are colored by hierarchical dynamics such as uncertainty absorption and withholding bad news.

The Importance of Deference Downward

HROs work to prevent unwanted outcomes such as those experienced by NASA. They are mindful of the dangers when command and control principles tend to "maintain the rungs of the work system's authority ladder; design engineers at the top, licensed reactor operators next, system or field engineers next, maintenance specialists below them, and those in staff and support functions at the bottom."[33] The problem is that the authority hierarchy does not correspond reliably with the knowledge hierarchy. When the status hierarchy outclasses the knowledge hierarchy in a nuclear plant, expertise is often overlooked because it is disguised by dirty coveralls and greasy hands. "Engineering separates itself from the hands-on work of operations, which separates itself from maintenance in a downward spiral from 'mind' to 'hand' to dirty overalls and greasy hands."[34] HROs make an effort to see what people with greasy hands know.

Diablo Canyon is a good example of deference downward. When its number two reactor shut down automatically, "the plant manager stayed out of the control room and relied on 'root cause' analyses by his senior people who, in turn, relied upon their subordinates."[35] Mathilde Bourrier describes a structure of this kind in outage planning at one of the nuclear power plants she studied. She noted that there was neither a detailed plan nor a special structure to deal with the outage. Instead, the most important characteristic was "the formal delegation of power to craft personnel supported by a nearly complete availability of top management at all times. By being a very flexible and adaptive organization, any problem can rapidly receive the attention it requires at all levels of the organization."[36] This mechanism permits the proficiency of the organization to come into play, provides checks and balances through oversight, and allows sequentially higher-level managers to take control of decisions should events begin to unravel.

Deference to Expertise Rather Than Experts

We prefer the concept of "expertise" to the concept of the "expert" because we want to preserve the crucial point that expertise is relational.[37] Expertise is an assemblage of knowledge, experience, learning, and intuitions that is seldom embodied in a single individual. And even if expertise appears to be confined to a single individual, that expertise is evoked and becomes meaningful only when a second person requests it, defers to it, modifies it, or rejects it. To defer to expertise is to act the way people on aircraft carriers do when they practice heedful interrelating.[38] Expertise resides in the heed with which people view their inputs as *contributions* rather than as solitary acts, *represent* the system within which their contributions and those of others interlock to produce outcomes, and *subordinate* their contributions to the well-being of the system, constantly mindful of what that system needs to remain productive and resilient.

Gene Rochlin found that emerging crises on aircraft carriers are often contained by informal networks.[39] When events get outside normal operational boundaries, knowledgeable people self-organize into ad hoc networks to provide expert problem solving. These networks have no formal status and dissolve as soon as a crisis is over. Such networks allow for rapid pooling of expertise to handle events that are impossible to anticipate. The ability to come together informally as the situation demands increases the knowledge and actions that can be brought to bear on a problem. The result is that the organization has more skills and expertise to draw on. This flexible strategy for crisis intervention enables a system to deal with inevitable uncertainty and imperfect knowledge.

Expertise and Credibility

The more we dig into expertise, the more we see that it is not simply an issue of content knowledge. Nowhere is this more evident than in what Paul Schulman describes as the three key values at Diablo Canyon: credibility, trust, and attentiveness.[40] Of the three, credibility is the most salient in the context of expertise. Credibility is a mixture of mutual recognition of skill levels and legitimacy. Deference and credibility, oddly enough, can come from candid acknowledgment of the limits of one's knowledge, as in the following example:

> At Charles Station, Jack, a shift manager, talked about his experience at another station where four transformers "were failing one at a time." Although tests showed that "the equipment's OK, all we can say is, 'It didn't fail its test.' That doesn't mean that it's OK. Well, people don't like to hear that, right? They want you to tell them it's OK. And all I can tell you is that it's not bad, because it passed its test, because a test is limited on the things it can test for."[41]

This manager's doubts testify to his credibility even though they also bring bad news. The danger here is that bad news will be dismissed by discrediting the credible manager.

The Columbia Accident Investigation Board seems to have hit just the right note when it commented on expertise at NASA. "In highly uncertain circumstances, when lives were immediately at risk, management failed to defer to its engineers and failed to recognize that different data standards—qualitative, subjective, and intuitive—and different processes—democratic rather than protocol and chain of command—were more appropriate."[42] Deference to expertise is as much collective as it is individual. And it is as much a structural issue as it is an issue of process. When people examine a surprise, they turn to others in an effort to understand what the surprise means. This represents a subtle loosening of hierarchy in favor of expertise. The loosening is not triggered by an edict from the top. Instead, it emerges from a collective, cultural belief that the necessary capabilities lie somewhere in the system and that migrating problems will find them. This means that decisions migrate down, but they also migrate up. If people in HROs get into situations they don't understand, they're not scared to ask for help. In a macho world, asking for help or admitting that you're in over your head, is frowned upon. Good HROs see it as a sign of strength to know when you've reached the limits of your knowledge and know enough to ask for help.

Acting for Containment: A Summary

HROs do not ignore foresight and anticipation, but they are mindful of its limitations. Under the assumption that uncertainty is irreducible and that the sources of harm are limitless, HROs invest more of their resources to help people contain and bounce back from unexpected events after they begin to occur. Our discussion revealed the following lessons involving containment from the more effective HROs:

- Pay just as much attention to building capabilities to cope with errors that have occurred as to improving capabilities to plan and anticipate events before they occur.

- Develop capabilities for mindfulness, swift learning, flexible role structures, and quick size-ups.

- Adopt an organizationwide mind-set of cure as well as prevention. This means that people are attentive to knowledge and resources that relieve, lighten, moderate, reduce, and decrease surprises. People are willing to begin treating an anomaly even before they have made a full diagnosis. They do so in the belief that this action will enable them to gain experience

and a clearer picture of what they are treating. Unlike anticipation, which encourages people to think and then act, resilience encourages people to act while thinking or to act in
order to think more clearly. A commander tries different tactics to learn what the enemy can do. This is empirical fighting.
It is reactive. It's supposed to be.

- Encourage people to make knowledge about the system trans-
  parent and widely known. The more people know about the
  weaknesses of their system and how to manage them, the
  faster they can notice and correct problems in the making.

- Establish pockets of resilience through uncommitted resources
  such as informal networks of people who come together on an
  as-needed basis to solve sticky problems.

- Create a set of operating dynamics that shifts leadership to
  the people who currently seem more likely to have an answer
  to the problem at hand.

Chapter Summary

In this chapter, we have elaborated on two principles of containment—commitment to resilience and deference to expertise—that
enable HROs to develop practices that reduce unwanted outcomes
after an unexpected event has occurred.

Despite the best-laid plans, unexpected events often force organizations to be reactive rather than proactive. *Resilient* reacting
occurs when a system stretches and then returns to something re-
sembling its former shape. These adjustments are made possible by
large and varied response repertoires, competence in reassembling
existing practices into new combinations, intense sharing of information, and a well-developed ability to maintain emotional control
in the face of chaos. Resource slack is treated as an asset rather than
a liability. *Expert* reacting occurs when authority and expertise are
decoupled and decision making migrates to expertise rather than

rank. Expertise resides as much in relationships as in individuals, meaning that interrelationships, interactions, conversations, and networks embody it. HROs are careful not to equate expertise solely with a single expert. HROs also look downward toward the front line to find credible expertise.

In the next chapter, we show how you can assess the extent to which you are now functioning like an HRO.

5

Assessing Your Capabilities
for Resilient Performance

To this point in the book, we have analyzed the nature of high reliability organizations by applying the five main principles of mindfulness. In the final three chapters, we turn to the question of how to implement the results of this analysis and become more like an HRO.

In this chapter, we describe nine audits that will help you and your organization become more alert to the dimension of mindfulness and mindlessness in your own work and system. The purpose of these questions is to help you detect moments when you or your organization are working on automatic pilot and those more mindful moments when you tend to treat preexisting labels, categories, and contexts as less well known and more in need of updating. The questions are also intended to help you develop more awareness of how to institutionalize mindfulness by spotting analogues of the five HRO principles in your own firm. These audits are the first step toward creating a greater number of mindful moments.

The Value of Conscious Audits

Winston Churchill provides a good example of the kind of self-conscious auditing we are concerned with in this chapter. During World War II, Churchill made the terrible discovery that Singapore was much more vulnerable to a Japanese land invasion than he first thought. Reflecting on this unexpected discovery, Churchill commented in his history of the war, "I ought to have known. My advisors ought to have known and I ought to have been told, and I ought to have asked."[1] Churchill's audit consisted of four questions: Why didn't I know? Why didn't my advisors know? Why wasn't I told? Why didn't I ask? Just imagine what would happen if, after a disruptive event, people used Churchill's protocol to discuss it. Such a discussion would sensitize everyone to the nature of mindfulness and to the early stages of an unexpected event.

Here is a situation similar to Churchill's. On March 6, 1987, the ferry boat *Herald of Free Enterprise* capsized and sank within five minutes of leaving the dock at Zeebrugge, Belgium, with its bow doors open. The tragedy resulted in the loss of 193 lives. As with any vessel, there were several standing orders. Order 01.09, "Ready for Sea," reads, "Heads of Departments are to report to the Master immediately if they are aware of any deficiency which is likely to cause their departments to be unready for sea in any respect at the due sailing time. In the absence of any such report the Master will assume, at the due sailing time, that the vessel is ready for sea in all respects."[2] What is interesting here is that this standing order violates two of Churchill's four requirements. It violates the requirement that his advisors should have informed him, and it violates the requirement that he should have inquired of them. Robert Allinson puts the point this way:

> Order 01.09 would seem to be worded in such a way as both not to require those in a position to know to make a report and not to require those to whom a report is being made to ask for the conclusions of a report. The total absence of a report is taken to be sufficient that the ship is ship shape. Thus, this order is two steps away from Churchill's requirements. It would not even meet his requirements if it were to state that a report must be made. It would further require that there must be a request for such a report in the case that there was a failure to report.[3]

The problem with the standing order is obvious but tricky. If you hear nothing, you assume that things are safe. But another reason you may hear nothing is that things are *not* safe. The reporter may be incapacitated—a signal of great danger. This was the case with the *Herald of Free Enterprise*. The seaman who was responsible for closing the bow doors had fallen asleep in his cabin and did not wake up until he was thrown out of his bunk as the boat capsized. What does it mean in a mindful organization when there is no news? Does it mean that things are going well, that they are going poorly, or that it is unclear how things are going? An organization's "default" answer tells us something important about the degree to which the organization is mindful. And that, in turn, begins to tell us something about how well or how poorly it is likely to deal with the unexpected.

These are the kinds of questions that are the focus of this chapter.

The Audits and How to Use Them

Before we proceed with the audits, remember that mindful moments are more important if you work in contexts that are dynamic, ill structured, ambiguous, or unpredictable. If the context is more stable, action that is less mindful, and more routine is more appropriate and often less costly. The trouble with this rule of thumb is that it is not nearly as neat and tidy as it sounds. We all like to have our expectations confirmed, which means we all are likely to overestimate how stable our world is. Hence we act less mindfully more often than we should. That is why the unexpected so often gets the best of us. It goes undetected longer until it becomes more formidable and disruptive.

In the following pages, we look separately at mindfulness and the five principles that produce it. We introduce each set of questions by first reviewing the ideas and concepts that generated them. We do this so you can see why the items are worded the way they are and which aspects of mindfulness are being assessed. More important, since you will know the general ideas that lie behind specific items, you can use those ideas to write additional questions that may be more sensitive to the specifics of your own firm. The goal of this exercise is to help you see how you stack up in comparison to best practices in HROs. If customizing some of the items helps you make that assessment, be sure to do so.

We encourage you to fill out these audits and then ask others in your company to do the same. But before you discuss the results, go one step further. Try to predict *in advance* how the other units, functions, specialties, and locations within your own organization will rate the items (and ask them to do the same for you). Then compare answers. There are scoring guidelines at the bottom of each questionnaire to help you interpret your answers. Later we will explain in more detail how to interpret and use the results. For now, answer the questions for yourself and imagine how members of your work unit, department, or executive team might answer them.

Audit 5.1: What Do You Count On?
A General Starting Point

Here is the background for the set of items in Audit 5.1.

Organizations are set apart and referred to as *reliability-centered or reliability-seeking* because they remain failure-free under conditions that threaten production and safe operations. These organizations are distinctive precisely because they let fewer unexpected events blow up into crises. People in HROs are just like people in other organizations in the sense that they don't know beforehand what will go wrong. But unlike people in most other organizations, they have a good sense of what needs to go right and a clearer understanding of the factors that might signal that things are unraveling. Because people in HROs are united in this awareness, everyone is alert to unanticipated possibilities. Hence they become aware of unforeseen events sooner, when it is easier to correct deviations and act more quickly when there are more possible courses of action.

Effective HROs have a broader, shared understanding of what it is that people want to go right and how it might go wrong. The question of how well people understand these things is as good a place as any to start your audit of mindfulness. To move toward a more mindful system, you need to enlarge what people monitor, ex-

Audit 5.1: A Starting Point for Assessing Your Firm's Mindfulness

How well do the following statements characterize your organization? For each item, circle the number that best reflects your conclusion: 1 = not at all, 2 = to some extent, 3 = a great deal.

1. There is a sense of susceptibility to the unexpected throughout the organization.   1   2   3

2. Everyone feels accountable for reliability.   1   2   3

3. Leaders pay as much attention to managing unexpected events as they do to achieving formal organizational goals.   1   2   3

4. People at all levels of our organization worry constantly about misspecifying events.   1   2   3

5. People at all levels of our organization worry constantly about misidentifying events.   1   2   3

6. People at all levels of our organization worry constantly about misunderstanding events.   1   2   3

7. We spend time identifying how our activities could potentially harm all our stakeholders.   1   2   3

8. There is widespread agreement among the firm's members on what we don't want to go wrong.   1   2   3

9. There is widespread agreement among the firm's members about how things could go wrong.   1   2   3

Scoring: Add the numbers. If you score higher than 17, the *mindful infrastructure* in your firm is exemplary. If you score between 11 and 17, your firm is on its way to building a *mindful infrastructure*. Scores lower than 11 suggest that you should be actively considering how you can immediately improve your firm's capacity for mindfulness.

pect, and fear. Paul Schulman's studies of nuclear power and electrical grid management organizations provide strong support for the idea that "all else being equal, the more people in an organization who are concerned about the misidentification, mis-specification, and misunderstanding of things, the higher the reliability that organization can hope to achieve."[4]

Be sure to notice that we keep using the word *enlarge* rather than the word *focus*. We steer clear of the word *focus* because it suggests a process of exclusion: *Focus* excludes; *enlarge* includes. Recall that people in HROs tend to be inclusive in the clues they use to monitor the health of the system as a whole. High reliability organizations are distinguished by the breadth of what people monitor, expect, and fear. Less breadth should mean more occasions for surprise and less reliability. Therefore, when you do an audit, listen for the word *focus* as a possible red flag.

Answers to the questions in Audit 5.1 will provide insight into whether people are conscious of potential problems and how open they are to finding out. Mindfulness increases as people become more conscious about the ways in which the system can be disrupted, what might go wrong, and who these disruptions are likely to harm. And when mindfulness increases, people are less likely to deny that unexpected surprises can happen or to rationalize away the potential consequences.

Audit 5.2: Appraising Tendencies Toward Mindlessness

Mindfulness conveys a mental orientation toward continually refining and differentiating categories, an ongoing willingness and capability to invent new categories that carve events into more meaningful sequences, and a more nuanced appreciation of context and ways to deal with it.[5] In contrast, a tendency toward mindlessness is characterized by a style of mental functioning in which people follow recipes, impose old categories to classify what they see, act with some rigidity, operate on automatic pilot, and mislabel unfamiliar new contexts as familiar old ones. A mindless mental style works to conceal problems that are worsening.

Mindlessness is more than a simple assessment of attention, preoccupation, or the factors that distract or interfere with people's attention. It is a deeper probe into how often people come into contact with the unexpected in their day-to-day activities, how much people expect that things will go as planned, and how strong their tendencies are either to solve or to ignore the disruptions that unexpected events produce. Instances of mindlessness occur when people confront weak stimuli, powerful expectations, and strong desires to see what they expect to see. Mindlessness is more likely

---

Audit 5.2: Assessing Your Firm's Vulnerability to Mindlessness

---

How well do the following statements describe your work unit, department, or organization? Circle the number that best reflects your conclusion: 1 = not at all, 2 = to some extent, 3 = a great deal.

1. Exceptions rarely arise in our work.   1   2   3

2. We encounter the same kinds of situations and   1   2   3
   problems day after day.

3. People in this organization have trouble getting all   1   2   3
   the information they need to do their work.

4. People are expected to perform their jobs in a   1   2   3
   particular way without deviations.

5. People often work under severe production pressures   1   2   3
   (time, costs, growth, profits, or other).

6. Pressures often lead people to cut corners.   1   2   3

7. People have little discretion to resolve unexpected   1   2   3
   problems as they arise.

8. Many people lack the skills and expertise they need   1   2   3
   to act on the unexpected problems that arise.

Scoring: Add the numbers. If you score higher than 16, the current potential for *mindlessness* is high, and you should be actively considering how you can immediately improve the capability for mindfulness. If you score between 10 and 16, the potential for *mindlessness* is moderate. Scores lower than 10 suggest a lower vulnerability to mindlessness.

---

when people face the same situations and problems day after day. To deal with the routine, people develop strong expectations of how the world will unfold and have a tendency to act on automatic pilot. Mindlessness is also likely when people are distracted, hurried, or overloaded. To deal with production pressures, people ignore discrepant cues and cut corners. Finally, mindlessness is more likely when people cannot do anything about what they see.

In fact, the close relationship between mindfulness and the action repertoire in HROs is a key to their effectiveness. Industrial sociologist Ron Westrum claims that organizations that are willing to act on specific surprises are also willing to acknowledge those surprises and think about them.[6] What this means is that when people bring new domains under their control and enlarge their ability to act on them, they also enlarge the range of issues they can notice in a mindful manner. For example, if people don't know how to learn from mistakes, they are not likely to notice many of their own mistakes, since they don't know what to do with them. If, however, they improve their capability to conduct thorough postmortems of what went wrong and to implement the lessons learned, they are likely to notice more mistakes because now they can do something about them. Conversely, if people are unable to act on surprises, it is not long before their "useless" observations of those surprises are also ignored or denied, with the result that events go unnoticed and can cumulate into bigger problems. Moreover, people with a limited action repertoire often impose old categories to classify what they see and mislabel unfamiliar new problems as familiar old ones so that they can act on them. For example, if firms traditionally decouple authority from responsibility and hold frontline people responsible for outcomes but don't give them the authority to ensure those outcomes, this limited way of working may well be imposed mindlessly on new fast-moving situations where high performance is possible only when responsibility and authority coincide. There's more than a grain of truth to the saying that when all you have is a hammer, every problem looks like a nail.

The questions in Audit 5.2 provide a window into your vulnerability to mindlessness because they reveal how strong people's tendencies are to ignore the disruptions that unexpected events cause.

Audit 5.3: Where You Need to Be Most Mindful

You need to be alert to the dimensions of mindfulness and mindlessness and how they permeate your work and your system. But you also need to be more attentive to situations where mindfulness can make a big difference. By that we mean situations where "ugly" surprises might be more likely to show up. In Chapter Three, you saw that surprises often surface at the human-system interface, such as maintenance-related work.[7] From the work of sociologist Charles Perrow we also know that unexpected events are likely to occur in

Audit 5.3: Assessing Where Mindfulness Is Most Required

Indicate whether you agree or disagree with each of the following statements about your work unit, department, or organization.

1. Work is accomplished through a number of sequential steps carried out in a linear fashion.   Agree   Disagree

2. Feedback and information on what is happening are direct and simply verified.   Agree   Disagree

3. The work process is relatively well understood.   Agree   Disagree

4. The work process *does not require* coordinated action.   Agree   Disagree

5. We can directly observe all the components in our "production" process.   Agree   Disagree

6. There are many different ways to produce our product or service (for example, items can be rerouted, schedules can be changed, and parts can be added later if delays or shortages occur).   Agree   Disagree

7. There is a lot of slack in our work process.   Agree   Disagree

8. In our work process, things don't have to be done right the first time because they can always be corrected.   Agree   Disagree

9. There is a lot of opportunity to improvise when things go wrong.   Agree   Disagree

Scoring: Count the number of "agree" and "disagree" responses. The greater the number of "disagree" responses, the *more* your system is *interactively complex and tightly coupled* and hence the more important it is to be mindful. Use these questions to begin thinking of the areas in your organization where mindfulness is crucial and ways to improve your capacity for mindfulness.

contexts that are *tightly coupled* and *interactively complex*.[8] *Coupling* concerns the degree to which actions in one part of the system directly and immediately affect other parts. A loosely coupled system is one where delays may occur and alternative pathways to completion are possible. A tightly coupled system has little slack, and a process or set of activities, once initiated, proceeds rapidly and irreversibly to a known or unknown conclusion. Tightly coupled systems have more time-dependent processes, so items must move continuously through the production process, and delays or storage of incomplete products is not possible.[9] For example, nuclear power generation and chemical processing are both highly time-dependent and precise processes.

Interactive complexity concerns how the different components or parts interact. For example, in a linear system such as an assembly line, components interact only with the components that precede or follow in some direct sequence. Moreover, the assembly process is relatively well understood. If a belt breaks and the line stops, the problem is fairly visible and comprehensible. Interactively complex systems possess a more elaborate set of interconnections and nonlinear feedback loops, some of which are hidden or impossible to anticipate. For example, nuclear power generation is not a set of independent, serial steps. Instead, it requires the coordination of numerous mechanical components by many operators. And despite years of operation, not all aspects of nuclear physics are completely understood.[10]

The rise of interconnected technologies, interconnected resource demands, and increased demands on attention mean that some parts of most organizational systems at one time or another move toward an interactively complex, tightly coupled state. Although mindfulness can't comprehend the incomprehensible, it can aid in the detection of early anomalies that can spiral into seemingly impossible outcomes. Answering the questions in Audit 5.3 will give you a sense of how tightly coupled and interactively complex your system is. If you get a feel for whether your system is loosely or tightly coupled and linear or interactively complex, you may be in a better position to know just how great the risk is of something unexpected and disastrous happening. If you have a tightly coupled, interactively complex system, you need to work on mindfulness—and soon.

Spotting the Five Principles in Your Organization

To this point, you have examined tendencies toward mindfulness and conditions where you might need it. The next set of questions focus on the five principles of mindfulness and probe your firm's current state with respect to a healthy preoccupation with failure, reluctance to simplify, sensitivity to operations, commitment to resilience, and deference to expertise. When you look for these HRO principles in your firm, you are looking at the capability of your system to generate reliable mindfulness.

Audit 5.4: Preoccupation with Failure

Failure in an HRO can be more catastrophic than is true for failure in your firm. Despite this difference in magnitude, the diagnostic value of failure is similar in both settings. In either setting, failure means that there was a lapse in detection: Someone somewhere didn't anticipate what and how things could go wrong. Something was not caught as soon as it could have been caught. And both mean that the system is not as healthy as it could be. An organization that is ignorant about failure, its location, genesis, and trajectory, is less mindful than it could be. But this deficiency need not be permanent. You can help the system be more alert to its failures, and you can do something about how the system handles failures and failure reporting. You can, for instance, articulate the types of things that should not fail and how they possibly could fail, help call attention to failures once they happen, articulate the consequences of continued denial of failure, uncover what happens to people when they report failures, seek similar failures elsewhere and benchmark how people manage them, spot the potential for failures in apparent successes, propose measures to detect failure systematically, and transmit memorable stories that preserve the lessons learned from failure. All these changes increase the capability for mindfulness.

Audit 5.4 can help you probe the degree to which your organization has a healthy preoccupation with failure. In performing this brief audit, you are also assessing the degree to which people are aware of mindfulness as a desirable outcome and of how it can be operationalized (for example, you notice how much time and effort people expend to understand their contexts). When it comes to mindfulness, it's good to feel bad and bad to feel good. This inverted logic derives from the many dangers of complacency that accompany success. To feel good may be to relax attentiveness and allow problems to accumulate undetected.

Audit 5.4: Assessing Your Firm's Preoccupation with Failure

How well do the following statements describe your work unit, department, or organization? For each item, circle the number that best reflects your conclusion: 1 = not at all, 2 = to some extent, 3 = a great deal.

1. We actively look for failures of all sizes and try to understand them.   1   2   3

2. When something unexpected occurs, we always try to figure out why our expectations were not met.   1   2   3

3. We treat near misses as information about the health of our system and try to learn from them.   1   2   3

4. We regard near misses as failures that reveal potential dangers rather than as successes that show our capability to avoid disaster.   1   2   3

5. We often update our procedures after experiencing a near miss.   1   2   3

6. If you make a mistake it is *not* held against you.   1   2   3

7. People report significant mistakes even if others do not notice that a mistake is made.   1   2   3

8. Managers actively seek out bad news.   1   2   3

9. People feel free to talk to superiors about problems.   1   2   3

10. People are rewarded if they spot potential trouble spots.   1   2   3

Scoring: Add the numbers. If you score lower than 12, you are preoccupied with *success* and should be actively considering how you can immediately improve your focus on *failure*. If you score between 12 and 20, you have a moderate preoccupation with success rather than a fully mindful preoccupation with failure. Scores higher than 20 suggest a healthy preoccupation with failure and a strong capacity for mindfulness.

Audit 5.5: Reluctance to Simplify

Part of what distinguishes high reliability organizations from other organizations is the extent to which they obsess about the question of what they ignore. But this difference is beginning to disappear. As global environments have become increasingly hard to anticipate and surprise has become more common, organizations of all kinds have become more mindful of what they ignore and more eager to learn how they can alter their processes of simplification. Their wariness and concern with blind spots is beginning to match the routine skepticism of HROs.

When you seek out the reluctance to simplify in your organization, you want to find how the system socializes people to make fewer assumptions, notice more, and ignore less. Probes into simplifications such as those presented in Audit 5.5 are probes into the existence of norms that acknowledge the reality of surprise and convey messages such as "take nothing for granted" and "don't get into something without a way out." But those items also assess the capability to look outside the confines of current expectations, to question and restrain temptations to simplify—capabilities cultivated by a *requisite variety* in human thought and action. Requisite variety is encouraged through diverse checks and balances that come from adversarial reviews, committees and meetings, frequent job rotation and retraining, and the selection of employees with nontypical prior experience.

Divergence in viewpoints provides the group with a broader set of assumptions and sensitivity to a greater variety of inputs, both of which are the antithesis of simplification. Unfortunately, diverse views tend to be disproportionately distributed toward the bottom of the organization, which means that the people most likely to catch unanticipated warning signals have the least power and argumentative skill to persuade others that the signal should be taken seriously. This isn't fatal if interpersonal skills and mutual respect are valued and if bullheadedness, hubris, and self-importance are not. Skeptics, curmudgeons, and iconoclasts are welcome in a mindful system, even if their presence is not always pleasurable. But this welcoming attitude exists only if there is strong shared sentiment that mindfulness is imperative to success. Short of that consensus, skeptics can have a rough time and find themselves dismissed with speed and enthusiasm.

Audit 5.5: Assessing Your Firm's Reluctance to Simplify

How well do following statements describe your work unit, department, or organization? For each item, circle the number that best reflects your conclusion: 1 = not at all, 2 = to some extent, 3 = a great deal.

1. People around here take nothing for granted.	1	2	3
2. Questioning is encouraged.	1	2	3
3. We strive to challenge the status quo.	1	2	3
4. People feel free to bring up problems and tough issues.	1	2	3
5. People generally deepen their analyses to better grasp the nature of the problems that arise.	1	2	3
6. People are encouraged to express different views of the world.	1	2	3
7. People listen carefully, and it is rare that someone's view goes unheard.	1	2	3
8. People are not attacked when they report information that could interrupt operations.	1	2	3
9. When something unexpected happens, people spend more time analyzing than advocating for their view.	1	2	3
10. Skeptics are highly valued.	1	2	3
11. People trust each other.	1	2	3
12. People show considerable respect for one another.	1	2	3

Scoring: Add the numbers. If you score higher than 24, the potential to *avoid simplification* is strong. If you score between 15 and 24, the potential to avoid simplification is moderate. Scores lower than 15 suggest that you should be actively considering how you can immediately improve your capabilities to prevent simplification in order to improve your firm's capacity for mindfulness.

Audit 5.6: Sensitivity to Operations

HROs are less concerned with strategy, which we conventionally equate with the big picture of the future, than with the big picture in the moment. Diagnosing your firm's sensitivity to operations by probing into the directions set out in Audit 5.6 can help you appraise how prepared you are to avert the accumulation of small events that can grow into bigger problems.

Being sensitive to operations is a unique way to correct failures of foresight. A comprehensive view of current operations enables

Audit 5.6: Assessing Your Firm's Sensitivity to Operations

Indicate whether you agree or disagree with each of the following statements about your work unit, department, or organization.

1. On a day-to-day basis, there is always someone who is paying attention to what is happening.   Agree   Disagree

2. Should problems occur, someone with the authority to act is always accessible to people on the front lines.   Agree   Disagree

3. Supervisors readily pitch in whenever necessary.   Agree   Disagree

4. People have discretion to resolve unexpected problems as they arise.   Agree   Disagree

5. During an average day, people interact often enough to build a clear picture of the current situation.   Agree   Disagree

6. People are always looking for feedback about things that aren't going right.   Agree   Disagree

7. People are familiar with operations beyond their own job.   Agree   Disagree

8. We have access to a variety of resources whenever unexpected surprises crop up.   Agree   Disagree

9. Managers constantly monitor workloads and reduce them when they become excessive.   Agree   Disagree

Scoring: Count the number of "agree" and "disagree" responses. The greater the number of "disagree" responses, the less the *sensitivity to operations*. Use these questions to begin thinking of ways to improve your sensitivity to operations and capacity for mindfulness.

organizations to catch most of the small errors and mistakes that would normally go unnoticed and be left to cumulate. The readiness to make large numbers of small adjustments keeps errors from accumulating. This reduces the likelihood that any one error will become aligned with another and interact with it in ways not previously anticipated.

You can help your system be more sensitive to operations by appraising the extent to which leaders and managers maintain continuous contact with the operating system or front line and the extent to which they are accessible when important situations develop. To what extent is there ongoing group interaction and information sharing about actual operations and workplace characteristics?

Audit 5.7: Commitment to Resilience

The central tension in the HRO literature is that once an error starts to amplify in a system, that error may be the system's last trial. So people in HROs try to do everything they can to anticipate possible failure modes. The reality, of course, is that humans and technologies are fallible. HROs accept the inevitability of error. This acceptance shifts attention from the ideal of error prevention to the more realistic goal of error containment.

Like HROs, your organization probably tries to prevent or anticipate surprises, but equally important is the question of how well prepared your system is to *manage* the unexpected when it does happen. We focus on the word *manage* to make it clear that people deal with surprises not only through anticipation, by weeding them out in advance, but also through resilience, by responding to them as they occur. Resilience is about bouncing back from errors and about coping with surprises in the moment. The capability for resilience, even if it is not exercised, aids diagnosis and detection of unwarranted simplifications and a cumulative trend in a series of errors. It is achieved through the use of expert networks, an extensive action repertoire, and skills with improvisation—resources that are

Audit 5.7: Assessing Your Firm's Commitment to Resilience

How well do the following statements describe your work unit, department, or organization? For each item, circle the number that best reflects your conclusion: 1 = not at all, 2 = to some extent, 3 = a great deal.

1.	Resources are continually devoted to training and retraining people to operate the technical system.	1	2	3
2.	People have more than enough training and experience for the kind of work they do.	1	2	3
3.	This organization is actively concerned with developing people's skills and knowledge.	1	2	3
4.	This organization encourages challenging "stretch" assignments.	1	2	3
5.	People around here are known for their ability to use their knowledge in novel ways.	1	2	3
6.	There is a concern with building people's competence and response repertoires.	1	2	3
7.	People have a number of informal contacts that they sometimes use to solve problems.	1	2	3
8.	People learn from their mistakes.	1	2	3
9.	People rely on one another.	1	2	3
10.	Most people have the skills to act on the unexpected problems that arise.	1	2	3

Scoring: Add the numbers. If you score higher than 20, the *commitment to resilience* is strong. If you score between 12 and 20, the commitment to resilience is moderate. Scores lower than 12 suggest that you should be actively considering how you can immediately begin building resilience and the capacity for mindfulness.

probed in Audit 5.7. Probes into your firm's commitment to resilience are probes into learning, knowledge, and capability development. Earlier in this chapter, we suggested that a major source of limited perception is a limited action repertoire. Expanding people's general knowledge and technical capabilities improves their abilities both to see problems in the making and to deal with them. Commitment to resilience is also evident in a capacity to use knowledge in unexpected ways. This capacity in your organization might be evident in informal networks of people who self-organize to solve problems, in enthusiasm to share expertise and novel solutions across unit boundaries, and in continual investments in improving technical systems, procedures, reporting processes, and employee attentiveness.

Audit 5.8: Deference to Expertise

In our analysis of high reliability organizing in Chapter Three, we confronted the paradox that the adoption of plans and standard procedures to reduce unexpected problems sometimes makes those problems worse. In the face of such a possibility and in response to changes in the tempo of demands, HROs shift their decision dynamics, authority structures, and functional patterns. There is a growing recognition that all organizations will require the same potential for flexible response in order to cope with diverse and rapidly changing competitive circumstances.

An audit of the extent to which your firm defers to expertise is more than a simple assessment of delegation or the extent to which decision rights are disseminated to people lower down in the hierarchy. It is a deeper probe into the extent to which people structure their attention. Recall from Chapter Four that effective HROs enact a more flexible decision-making structure when something goes wrong. They loosen the designation of who the "important" decision maker is in order to allow decision making and problems to migrate to the person or team with expertise in that choice-problem combination. Recall also that decisions migrate down as well as up. When tasks are highly interdependent and time is compressed, decisions migrate down to people at the point of problem sensing. Decisions migrate up when events are unique, have potential for very serious consequences, or have political or career ramifications that require organizational experience or familiarity that is more often found at higher than lower levels. Probes into your firm's deference to expertise are probes into accountability, respon-

Audit 5.8: Assessing the Deference to Expertise in Your Firm

How well do the following statements describe your work unit, department, or organization? For each item, circle the number that best reflects your conclusion: 1 = not at all, 2 = to some extent, 3 = a great deal.

1. People are committed to doing their job well.   1   2   3
2. People respect the nature of one another's job   1   2   3
   activities.
3. If something out of the ordinary happens, people   1   2   3
   know who has the expertise to respond.
4. People in this organization value expertise and   1   2   3
   experience over hierarchical rank.
5. In this organization, the people most qualified to   1   2   3
   make decisions make them.
6. People typically "own" a problem until it is resolved.   1   2   3
7. It is generally easy to obtain expert assistance when   1   2   3
   something comes up that we don't know how to handle.

Scoring: Add the numbers. If you score higher than 14, the *deference to expertise* is strong. If you score between 8 and 14, the deference to expertise is moderate. Scores lower than 8 suggest that you should be actively thinking of ways to improve the deference to expertise and capacity for mindfulness.

sibility, and broad awareness of where to go for help. Probing in the directions captured in Audit 5.8 provides a more systematic appraisal of the deference to expertise in your organization and should give you insight into your capability to localize problems and limit their spread.

Audit 5.9: The Mindfulness Organizing Scale

If you're like most organizations, you want to rapidly become reliable and improve your performance. But all too often there is limited time for improving. Conducting the series of audits contained in Audits 5.1 through 5.8 will give you a deep and broad sense of your organization's tendencies toward mindfulness and your capacities for organizing in ways to bring it about. But doing that will also take time—time that you may not have available immediately. A more economical audit, the Mindfulness Organizing Scale (MOS), is captured in Audit 5.9.[11] The probes contained in the MOS capture specific behaviors that we see in more highly reliable organizations. The beauty of the MOS lies not only in its succinctness but also in its utility. Vanderbilt researcher Tim Vogus studied medication misadministrations and patient falls in hospital nursing units and found that nursing units that reported higher scores on the MOS also reported significantly lower rates of medication errors and patient falls.[12] The MOS should give you a compact way to figure out whether people in your firm are acting in ways that are consistent with HRO principles. It should also give you a sense of where reliable performance is most likely to show up.

Interpreting the Audits and Using the Results

An audit usually stirs up a system. When you ask questions such as those presented in this chapter, people begin to pay attention to the issues implied by the questions. They talk about these topics. They refine their answers. They find themselves saying, "I wish I'd said . . ." It's pretty hard not to have these extended reactions when your attention has been drawn to a topic.

By their very nature, then, audits help create readiness. But readiness for what? In our case, there are several answers. First, the audits should help you become more comfortable imagining the unexpected as it has become an increasing part of the everyday. Second, they should provide a motive to benchmark your firm against the high reliability organization, which relies heavily on mindfulness to manage the unexpected and maintain relatively error-free performance. Third, the audits will give you an inventory of your daily practices and reveal the extent to which your practices incorporate the five principles of mindfulness. The intention is to help you increase your capability for mindfulness as a means to manage the unexpected.

Audit 5.9: The Mindfulness Organizing Scale

How well do the following statements describe your work unit, department, or organization? For each item, circle the number that best reflects your conclusion: 1 = not at all, 2 = to some extent, 3 = a great deal.

1. We have a good "map" of each person's talents and skills.	1	2	3
2. We talk about mistakes and ways to learn from them.	1	2	3
3. We discuss our unique skills with each other so that we know who has relevant specialized skills and knowledge.	1	2	3
4. We discuss alternatives as to how to go about our normal work activities.	1	2	3
5. When discussing emerging problems with coworkers, we usually discuss what to look out for.	1	2	3
6. When attempting to resolve a problem, we take advantage of the unique skills of our colleagues.	1	2	3
7. We spend time identifying activities we do not want to go wrong.	1	2	3
8. When errors happen, we discuss how we could have prevented them.	1	2	3
9. When a crisis occurs, we rapidly pool our collective expertise to attempt to resolve it.	1	2	3

Scoring: Add the numbers. If you score higher than 17, your firm's *mindful organizing* practices are strong. If you score between 11 and 17, your firm's mindful organizing practices are moderate. Scores lower than 11 suggest that you should be actively thinking of ways to improve your firm's mindful organizing practices.

If you increase your capability for mindfulness, many untoward consequences of the unexpected can be stopped before they get started. So we want you to feel more willing to grapple with the unexpected rather than avoid it, more willing to grapple with the unexpected mindfully rather than mindlessly, and more willing to benchmark on HROs as the guide for how to deal mindfully with the unexpected. By undertaking the audits, particularly if many people are part of the process, you can help enlarge your organization's mindfulness about its mindful qualities. When you exchange your observations, you will generate a richer picture of your system as you seek to understand the reasons for differences in your observations. Use the following questions to guide your debrief:

- How did you answer the questions posed in the audit?
- How did others answer the questions posed in the audit?
- To what extent did your assessment of other units match their assessment and vice versa?
- What did you not find that you expected to find?
- What did you find that you did not expect to find?
- What surprised you?

Remember the importance of surprise. Feelings of surprise are diagnostic because they are a solid cue that one's model of the world is flawed.

Four Issues to Examine

When you evaluate the responses to the audit items, look at four issues.

How Much Do People Agree? To what extent do people's assessments match across your organization? In the best case, similarities in responses across hierarchical levels, units, and functions will give you an integrated big picture similar to that found in the best-prepared HROs; in the worst case, the emerging picture will be fragmented, with people at certain levels or in particular functions or units giving answers that suggest they have a rich set of mindful processes in place and others giving answers that suggest that mindlessness is more the norm. You probably show tendencies toward both mindlessness and mindfulness. But do you exhibit them at the right places? Are you mindless in environments that are stable and predictable, and mindful in environments that are dynamic and unpredictable?

Look for audits with high variation of the scores. This means that people do not agree on that characteristic of the work unit, department, or organization. Where answers differ, consider the reasons for these differences and their implications. Disagreement is often a signal that something is being overlooked. So it is worthwhile to air the reasons for these differences in opinion because individuals with different ideas may have insights that no one else has. What is important is to get these differences into the open, especially if people provide credible evidence in support of their assessment. That clears the air of wishful thinking.

What Are You Good At? Are you consistently better at anticipation (the first three processes of mindfulness) than at containment (the last two processes)? You would expect that to occur in rational organizations, obsessed with planning. And because the value of building resilience and developing flexible decision processes is often underestimated in most organizations, it is natural to expect the latter two processes to be your poorest. Are they? If not, you're on your way to being a more mindful organization. Rank the five processes according to what you are best and worst at doing. Is your culture what is holding that ranking in place? Compare the rankings written by the topmost persons in the hierarchy with those written by the bottommost. Does the top see what the bottom sees? Is bad news reaching the top? Is there unexpected good news? Is the organization actually more mindful than the folks at the top believe? Tell them so.

Which unit, function, or department appears to perform better than others on each of the five processes? Pay particular attention to units that seem to have scored well, since this can signal that they have learned some important lessons about how to achieve mindfulness—lessons that can be shared with the rest of the firm.

What Is Dismaying? Ask your coworkers what dismayed and alarmed them when they saw the results. If nothing is dismaying or alarming, ask yourself why not? The lack of dismay could be a sign of deadly complacency with the status quo and could represent a major barrier to enacting a more mindful infrastructure.

Where Could You Be More Mindful? Use the audit results to diagnose areas that need specific attention and formulate an action plan. As a group, decide what you can do to improve the capacity for mindfulness. Look to other groups or units that appear to have mastered the process for help in deciding on a course of action (we introduce specific remedies in Chapters Six and Seven from which you can choose). Assign a champion for the process. Once you decide what you want to change, you also need to determine how progress on these fronts will be measured—change in what? What is a significant time interval in which to see some change? Make sure that someone is appointed to monitor and report progress on accomplishing any change to your mindful infrastructure.

Repeating the Audits

When should people in your group repeat the audits? You can use the items in the audits as part of an ongoing monitoring process and of course should add items as your experience with and understanding of your system grow. For example, pick a "failure of the month" to scrutinize. Assess where you stand on the processes as you work your way through your analysis. What happens the next month as a consequence of treating the first failure more mindfully? Slippage (which occurs as scores start to change in the wrong direction) can indicate a drift away from mindfulness and can signal areas that may need attention and reinforcement.

People in HROs spend the bulk of their time reaccomplishing and reinforcing efforts to build a mindful infrastructure. They understand that mindful processes unravel pretty fast. The uncertain technology and environment warrant nothing less than an ongoing effort. We believe that the same holds true for you.

In today's context, it makes sense for any organization to become more like an HRO. Today's business conditions involve increased competition, higher customer expectations, reduced cycle
time, and tight interdependence. These changes produce environments that are almost as harsh, risky, and unforgiving as those that
HROs confront. That being the case, organizations that confront
an HRO-like environment with HRO-like processes should have
more success at learning and adaptation than those that don't.

Chapter Summary

In this chapter, we converted the lessons learned from the study of
high reliability organizations into sets of questions to help you assess your firm's mindfulness, tendencies toward mindlessness, and
current infrastructure to combat mindlessness. We suggested that
you customize the audits for your unique context and administer
them widely. The information you gain from administering the audits across hierarchies, specialties, and functions is a prime source
of information about what people know about their system, the
ways in which it can fail, and the defenses in place to prevent surprises from getting out of hand.

Implicit in this discussion were suggestions for beginning to institutionalize mindfulness and the processes that contribute to it. Of
course, there are many techniques that relate directly or indirectly
to managing unexpected events, such as effective people management practices, selection, training, skill checks, design of procedures, and administrative mechanisms. It is not within the scope of
this book to review all possible techniques. Rather, our focus is on
operating practices that relate directly to the five elements that create a mindful infrastructure and enable HROs to be more aware of
their own capabilities, what they face, and what that might mean.
The next two chapters develop these ideas further.

6

Organizational Culture: Institutionalizing Mindfulness

The brief period after you have finished the mindfulness audits is a lot like the period right after the chaos of battle on a battlefield. There are truths lying around everywhere that may be picked up for the asking. This is the moment of learning. But it won't be long before candor gives way to moments of normalizing that protect reputations, decisions, and styles of managing. As soon as official stories get "straightened out" and repeated, learning stops. The same is likely to be true of the moments of truth stirred up by an audit of mindfulness. HROs manage to stretch those moments. The purpose of these final two chapters is to help you stretch your own moments of candor so you can see ways to improve on what the audits uncovered.

This chapter is about corporate culture—what holds your group together, sets its prevailing tone, and may need to be changed if mindfulness is to be sustained. True, the only person you can change is yourself. But as you become more mindful, you can champion these behaviors, model them for others, and benefit from them yourself. (We focus on these personal implications in Chapter Seven.) Prevailing cultures shape your actions as well as how your acts are interpreted. This means that even the best-intentioned small pockets of mindful action can get swept away by prevailing, socially approved mindlessness. You'll see an example of this when we discuss excess deaths in the pediatric cardiac unit of the Bristol Royal Infirmary. If, however, people begin to practice mindfulness, and if they begin to expect mindfulness from one another, approve those who take mindfulness seriously, and disapprove those who don't, they will be moving toward a set of norms that hold mind-fulness in place. And that, in turn, will make it a whole lot easier for you personally to act mindfully and resiliently.

Taking Stock and Moving Forward

You've seen the Cerro Grande firefighting crew organize in ways that made it harder for them to keep up with an increasingly active fire. You've seen that expectations impose substantial blinders that are removed only by continuous, mindful efforts that counteract misperceptions. You've seen that mindfulness is about attentiveness and updating to get the situation right. You've seen that five prin-ciples provide the foundation and guidelines that HROs use when they build their own locally rational practices.

As a result of your audits, you've spotted some attitudes and be-havior that keep you from being more mindful. In that sense, you've spotted some resemblance between your group and the Cerro Grande fire team. But you've also spotted some current attitudes and behav-iors in your group that promote mindfulness. Those unnoticed assets are more crucial to managing the unexpected than you may have realized. The chances are that you didn't realize they were so impor-tant, and neither did the other people in the group. So now you find yourself with a list of behaviors and processes that need to be added, deleted, and reaffirmed.

What you need to do next is modify what people expect from one another by way of mindful updating. This modification is not just a change in how people think; it is also a change in how they feel and act. You need people to absorb the lessons of mindfulness at an emotional level so that they will express approval when others hold certain beliefs and act in certain ways. For example, people need to feel strongly that it's good to speak up when they make a mistake, good to spot flawed assumptions, good to focus on a per-sistent operational anomaly. They need to expect support for these acts when they do them, and they need to offer support when someone else does them. Likewise, you need to attach disapproval to actions that undermine mindfulness. For example, people need to agree that it's bad to refrain from asking for help, bad to let success go to their heads, bad to ignore lower-ranking experts. They need to express key values as much through disapproval as through approval.

As people make these kinds of changes, a new culture begins to emerge. The culture takes the form of a new set of expectations and standards (norms) and a new urgency that people live up to them. In the case of mindfulness, they start living up to the expectation that everyone in the organization should work mindfully, that there are no exceptions, and that those who think otherwise will be nudged from the center of the group to the periphery. An organizational culture emerges from a set of expectations that matter to people. Powerful social forces such as inclusion, exclusion, praise, positive feelings, social support, isolation, care, indifference, excitement, and anger are the means by which people make things matter for one another. All of us are products of our relationships, our mutual accommodations with other people, and the respectful interactions that define us. This means that we shape the cultures that in turn shape us. Expectations and norms pull behaviors from us that we are more or less proud of, draw attention to certain values and away from other ones, and influence our priorities.

In the remainder of this chapter, we first lay out an overview of what we mean by culture. In brief, culture is both a way of seeing and a way of not seeing. Second, we translate the general picture of culture into a more specific picture that is focused on mindfulness by exploring James Reason's notion of an informed culture. And finally, we show, using the example of the Bristol Royal Infirmary, how a less mindful, less informed culture mismanages the unexpected, with fatal results.

The Form of Organizational Culture

One of the earliest discussions of organizational culture was Barry Turner's work in the early 1970s. It remains one of the clearest descriptions of culture and its importance for organizing. In Turner's words:

Part of the effectiveness of organizations lies in the way in which they are able to bring together large numbers of people and imbue them for a sufficient time with a sufficient similarity of approach, outlook and priorities to enable them to achieve collective, sustained responses which would be impossible if a group of unorganized individuals were to face the same problem. However, this very property also brings with it the dangers of a collective blindness to important issues, the danger that some vital factors may be left outside the bounds of organizational perception.[1]

In other words, culture is the source of an economical, powerful "similarity of approach." The "similarity" results from shared values, norms, and perceptions that are the raw materials of culture. When these raw materials are held in common, the resulting "shared expectations associated with clusters of roles in an organizational group tend to encourage members of the group to bring certain assumptions to the task of decision making within the organization, and to operate with similar views of rationality."[2] It is these shared expectations, assumptions, and similar views of rationality that constitute an integrated culture that can either encourage or discourage mindfulness. Culture can encourage blind spots.

That aspects of culture are *shared* seems obvious, but Stanford University researchers Debra Meyerson and Joanne Martin have pointed out that culture is not monolithic and defined by meanings that are harmonious and shared (this is known as an *integration* view of culture). When you describe culture as shared, you ignore the fact that there are *also* subcultures that are in conflict with one another (this is known as a *differentiation* view of culture) and individuals whose interpretations are irreconcilable and difficult to put boundaries around (this is known as a *fragmentation* view of culture). Each form of culture handles ambiguity differently: integration denies it, differentiation selectively clarifies it, and fragmentation accepts it.[3] In a mindful culture, all three forms of culture are present.

There are costs and benefits to the way each form of culture handles ambiguity. Cultures that are integrative tend to deny ambiguity. Cultures that are differentiated and fragmented tend to accept ambiguity, which enables them to register more variety. HROs tend toward the latter pattern even though at times this makes it harder to disseminate signals of trouble. While HROs make an effort to develop an integrated culture focused on safe operations, they rely heavily on the distinctive subcultures associated with operators, engineers, and executives to detect a broader range of weak signals.[4]

We have placed more weight on fragmentation than on differentiation and more on differentiation than on integration. The reason we did this is because the environments that HROs face are typically more complex than the HRO systems themselves. Reliability and resilience lie in practices that reduce those differences in complexity. Wise practices either reduce environmental complexity or increase system complexity. Assuming that it is harder to change the environment than your system, we have highlighted ways you can improve sensing and acting when faced with complexity. Our recommendations boil down to this advice: *make your system more complicated*. That recommendation is based on a basic principle in system design called the principle of requisite variety.[5]

The principle of requisite variety means essentially that if you want to cope successfully with a wide variety of inputs, you need a wide variety of responses. If you have less variety than your inputs, the system could be destroyed. For example, consider the maxim "You have to fight fire with fire." In wildland firefighting, this is sometimes literally true. Conventional firefighting tools such as streams of water, removing surface fuels, dropping slurry from aircraft, heaping dirt on flames, or using evergreen boughs to beat out flames may be too simple and rigid to match the higher variety of fire behavior. In this case, firefighters fight complex fires with equally complex backfires in an effort to better match and manage what they face.

When we combine all three views of culture, we see that culture is never monolithic. Consensus, dissensus, and confusion *coexist*, which makes it tough to talk about "the" culture.[6] With all this complexity, it may seem that the idea of culture is more trouble than it's worth. We don't think so. We still need the idea so that we have a compact way to talk about "shared values (what is important) and beliefs (how things work) that interact with an organization's structures and control systems to produce behavioral norms (the way we do things around here)."[7] This is the "sufficient similarity of approach" that we saw back in Turner's definition of culture.

Analysts still differ on the question of whether culture should be understood as something an organization *is* (its beliefs, attitudes, and values) or whether culture should be understood as something an organization *has* (its practices and controls). While there is a grain of truth to both assumptions, James Reason and others argue that it is harder to change attitudes and beliefs directly than it is to change acting and doing, which can then lead to changes in thinking and believing.[8] Acting and doing are influenced by practices—policies and norms that, over time and in the context of group affiliations, shape attitudes and beliefs.[9] We think culture is something an organization has that eventually becomes something an organization is. Organizations act their way into what they become.

How Culture Develops

Of the many recent descriptions that attempt to capture key properties of cultures, Edgar Schein's is perhaps the best known. In Schein's view, culture is defined by six formal properties: (1) shared basic assumptions that are (2) invented, discovered, or developed by a given group as it (3) learns to cope with its problem of external adaptation and internal integration in ways that (4) have worked well enough to be considered valid and, therefore, (5) can be taught to new members of the group as the (6) correct way to perceive, think, and feel in relation to those problems.[10] The one addition that we would make to point 6 is that culture is as much about practices and actions as it is about mind-sets. When we talk about culture, therefore, we are talking about

- Assumptions that preserve lessons learned from dealing with the outside and the inside

- Values derived from these assumptions that prescribe how the organization should act

- Practices or ways of doing business

- Artifacts or visible markers that embody and give substance to the espoused values

Artifacts are the easiest to change, assumptions the hardest.

What Schein has spelled out in careful detail, people often summarize more compactly: culture is "how we do things around here." For our purposes, we modify that slightly and argue that culture is also "what we expect around here." Cultures affect both what people expect from one another internally (these expectations are often called norms) and what people expect from their dealings with the external environment of customers, competitors, suppliers, shareholders, and other stakeholders.[11] In either case, expectations take the form of agreements about appropriate attitudes and behaviors.

Culture affects how departures from expectations are detected, interpreted, managed, and used as pretexts for learning. What differs from group to group is the extent to which people agree on what is appropriate and how strongly they feel about the appropriateness of the attitude or behavior. If everyone feels strongly about the importance of a behavior, there is little latitude for deviation, and slight departures from the norm are dealt with swiftly and harshly. For instance, if a group of commuter pilots feel strongly that checklists are for "sissies," anyone who tries to use one unobtrusively is subject to ridicule. If, however, agreement is less widespread and people feel less passionate about the issue, there is a weaker norm around checklists, deviations are more commonplace, and this expectation will do little to hold the group together.

How Culture Controls

The key point to remember about values, culture, and expectations was first mentioned more than two decades ago by Thomas Peters and Robert Waterman in their best-seller *In Search of Excellence*. They argued that if people in an organization were committed to no more than three or four core values and if they internalized these values and shared them, top management could give these committed people wide latitude to make decisions because they would frame those decisions in a similar, preferred manner. The handful of key values would shape how people perceived an issue and how they acted. Hence an organization could gain the benefits of both centralization and decentralization if members were centralized on a handful of key values and then given autonomy on everything else. Peters and Waterman stated the point this way: "Autonomy is a product of discipline. The discipline ([instilled by] a few shared values) provides the framework. It gives people confidence (to experiment for instance) stemming from stable expectations about what really counts. . . . The discipline of a small number of shared values induces practical autonomy and experimentation throughout the organization."[12] A culture with three or four key values that have been converted into norms for appropriate behavior will be coordinated and resilient.

Thus culture is a key element in efforts to manage the unexpected mindfully. That assertion is both simple and complex. It is simple in the sense that the idea of culture itself is simple: "There is nothing magical or elusive about corporate culture. One has only to be clear about the specific attitudes and behaviors that are desired, and then to identify the norms or expectations that promote or impede them."[13] But culture is also complex. Figure 6.1 shows that there are many conditions that have to fall into place in order to produce clear norms and a strong culture. In particular, a culture of mindfulness, held together by norms of appropriate behavior, will not persist unless

- Top management conveys a clear preference for mindfulness in its beliefs, values, and actions
- Those top management actions and words are communicated credibly and consistently and remain salient for everyone
- Those communicated values are seen to be consistent rather than hypocritical and are felt strongly by the majority of people
- Bonuses, raises, promotions, and approval flow toward those who act mindfully and away from those who don't

That is a lot of contingencies—and lots of places where efforts to build a strong, mindful culture can get sidetracked.

Figure 6.1 Conditions That Create Corporate Culture

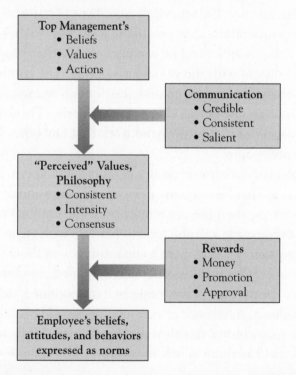

Here's an example of managing these contingencies successfully. It involves Herb Brown, captain of the carrier USS *Kennedy*. Several years ago, Brown's command style was the centerpiece of a television documentary that gave a "backstage" view of a functioning warship.[14] Brown's efforts to build a culture of high reliability on the carrier can be traced through the stages summarized in Figure 6.1, which you can also use to trace your own efforts to change culture. Brown's beliefs and values center on safety ("Let's do it by the numbers"), keeping people informed ("When I was nineteen and on a ship, no one ever told me anything, and I vowed never to repeat that"), and caring for his people ("I love them"). He communicates these values by frequent use of the public address system and face-to-face communication. In both settings, people see that he takes these values seriously. They also see that he is a credible and consistent communicator. Brown's views are salient because he continuously moves around the ship, practicing what he preaches. Brown makes his values visible, and he can also see whether people's actions are consistent with the values he supports. The combination of salient beliefs and credible communication has an impact on the perceptions of people farther down the hierarchy. Those perceptions are converted into meaningful work that embodies Brown's values and philosophy.

Credible, consistent expressions of values in Captain Brown's actions confirm that he is serious about what he says and does. If he is seen as serious, then the content of what he espouses becomes what the rank-and-file will also tend to practice with greater intensity and consistency. But if there is inconsistency in Brown's words and deeds, and if that inconsistency gets amplified by suspect communication, the people at lower ranks become confused, suspicious, and demoralized. As a result of such confusion and cynicism, the values that now control frontline action are more likely to be inconsistent, held without much conviction, and fragmented between subcultures.

There is one final step in the process of control that Captain Brown uses to shape culture. Regardless of the "perceived" values and philosophy, the captain still can have an effect on culture by who and what he rewards. Such things as promotions, awards, bonuses, appointments, praise for work done, conversation, addressing people by name, and temporary assignments all send signals to the entire ship regarding what is important. If the captain's early communications and later rewards are consistent with the beliefs and actions he initially promoted, these beliefs take hold and persist as institutionalized norms. In short, having passed several demanding interpersonal tests involving credibility, consistency, salience, consensus, intensity, and targets of reward, the resulting beliefs and values give the ship a "personality" that resembles the personality of the captain. That emerging culture is unique in the assumptions that generate expectations, the ways in which those expectations are monitored and revised, the degree to which the elements of the culture fit together (are integrated), and the extent to which the culture makes it easier or harder to sustain reliable performance and outcomes.

The subtlety in all of this is that the culture is not just about the sailors' specific beliefs on issues such as how much discretion should be left to pilots, how women aviators should be treated, what kinds of penalties should be handed down for first-time drug users, and so on. Those are content issues, and culture is more than content. It is about collective practices such as those that depend on organizational structures and systems.[15] Therefore, culture is not reflected just in the stance on specific issues. It is reflected also in the *way* "the stance itself is developed, reinforced, eroded, or altered by the various needs and interests that confront individuals and organizations."[16] Culture consists of characteristic ways of knowing and sensemaking. "*How* we develop expectations around here" is an expression of culture. On aircraft carriers, for example, one way they develop culture is by paying close attention to "lessons bought in blood." Tragedy is the occasion for culture change. Moments "bought in blood" occur when people test the edge of the performance envelope (for example, can we get recovery of aircraft down from fifty-second spacing between aircraft to forty-five seconds without a crash?) and institutionalize the results, good or bad, in revised practices and assumptions. "The way we develop expectations around here" can be done more or less mindfully, depending on whether risky work is monitored for early signs of failure, treated as a complex event, scrutinized from moment to moment, managed by making do, and executed by experts.

Culture is the style of work on the carrier, a style that includes development and alteration of "what we expect around here." Culture is about practices—practices of expecting, managing disconfirmations, sensemaking, learning, and recovering. Units translate the precepts of mindfulness in distinctive ways into their own locally rational, practical versions of mindful practices.

How Culture Can Be Changed

Culture change is hard, slow, and subject to frequent relapse. Edgar Schein is absolutely right when he counsels people to attempt culture change only when there is a specific problem to be solved and only when they can work with existing cultural strengths. He makes the point this way:

> Never start with the idea of changing culture. Always start with the issue the organization faces; only when those business issues are clear should you ask yourself whether the culture aids or hinders resolving the issues. Always think initially of the culture as your source of strength. It is the residue of your past successes. Even if some elements of the culture look dysfunctional, remember that they are probably only a few among a large set of others that continue to be strengths. If changes need to be made in how the organization is run, try to build on existing cultural strengths rather than attempting to change those elements that may be weaknesses.[17]

Culture is tough to change because different views of culture imply different strategies for change. An integration view suggesting that culture is monolithic calls for organizationwide, revolutionary change controlled by those in leadership positions. A differentiation view calls for changes that have local, subunit impact and treats organizationwide change as unlikely. A fragmentation view claims that all individuals are constantly changing and are changed by the cultures they live in. Fragmented changes tend to be issue-specific rather than subunit-specific or organization-specific. Unless you tackle all three, culture change is incomplete. For example, if you want people to speak up when they spot an error, this proposed change starts out as an intention to be shared by everyone, and it assumes a unified organization that will be responsive to leader-centered initiatives. But "speaking up" means different things in different units. And the issue of speaking up itself is ambiguous in that it is unclear what qualifies as an incident to be reported. Because of these complications, culture change often starts small, with a change in symbols or a change in behavior.

Change Through Symbols. You can initiate culture change with symbols, the "artifacts" we mentioned earlier. To change a symbol is to work backward in culture change. First you change the symbol, then newer values get articulated around the symbol and attached to it, and finally assumptions become aligned with the newer symbols and values. Basically, you start with easy changes as leverage for larger and deeper changes. Symbols may seem corny as a place to start, but don't slight them. They can be persistent reminders of what a culture stands for or could stand for. Gordon Bethune, the imaginative CEO who managed the turnaround of Continental Airlines, is a master of symbols. One of his early innovations was to promise all employees (all forty thousand of them) a bonus of $65 to be paid at the end of each month that Continental's on-time record placed it among the top five airlines nationwide according to the Department of Transportation's numbers.[18] Continental was dead last in on-time performance when the program was announced in January 1995. In February 1995, it was in fourth place, and the checks went out. In March, it was in first place for the first time in its history.

That is a story in itself. But the story we're interested in unfolded during a stop on the "road show" that saw Bethune visiting various field stations to explain his priorities. At a meeting in Newark, New Jersey, where he was extolling the bonuses, one employee stood up and said he could certainly understand how people such as gate agents, schedulers, mechanics, baggage handlers, and flight crews would get the bonus. But he couldn't understand why people such as reservation agents who merely answered phones and never laid a hand on a plane "should be getting a share of the dough." How was Bethune going to justify giving away money to people who never got near an airplane as part of their job? Bethune reached up his jacket sleeve, pulled off his watch, held it up, and asked the employee, "Which part of this watch don't you think we need?" The employee had no answer and sat down; the value of teamwork had just been made palpable. The image of a watch said more about teamwork, more vividly, than any laminated card with the word TEAMWORK splashed on it. Later Bethune drew the moral of the watch more explicitly:

> Every part of the watch is not only necessary but as important as every other part. Everybody thinks he or she is the hour hand—everybody thinks he or she is the most important part of the watch. That's just human nature. But for the watch to run, all the parts have to be working. And when you're dealing with human parts, the best way to keep all the parts running is to treat them well.[19]

The *artifact* of a watch suggested the *value* of pulling together and made people more receptive to the *assumption* that communities get things done. Bethune's wristwatch didn't change the culture. But seen and seen again there on the arm of a powerful CEO, the watch did unfreeze the prevailing beliefs about who mattered and who didn't. It was a compact symbol of preferred ways of working. It served as a credible, consistent, intense message from the CEO that fit what he had been saying in other venues. It was a portable, vivid symbol that could also be noted whenever employees looked at their own timepieces. It was a small win but also a durable win.

Change Through Acting into Values. Another small but influential pathway to culture change is to adopt the principle that people act their way into new values. If people perform some action publicly, irrevocably, and voluntarily, they tend to see themselves (and others tend to see them) as responsible for the action.[20] And if they feel responsible for an action, they feel some pressure to come up with plausible reasons why they chose to perform it, even if they were not aware of those reasons at the time. The reasons that are discovered after the fact could consist of recently discussed beliefs and assumptions that are consistent with the new culture. The context created by the perception that one's acts were public, irrevocable, and voluntary makes one more receptive to plausible reasons for the acts. If salient plausible reasons include newer values and assumptions that reflect a preferred direction of culture change, one is more likely to internalize those values. In short, if people feel as if they have chosen to take some action, they'll be receptive to explanations of why they did it.

For example, suppose that Gordon Bethune had said at one of his road show meetings, "We've got a very tough stretch ahead for the sales unit, and it will take pain and sacrifice to pull through. I understand that some of you may not feel up to this and want to work elsewhere in the corporation. I will approve those transfers. Let's break for lunch. If you want to continue with this change, come on back to this room for the afternoon session. If you want to work elsewhere in the corporation, please go to the Valencia Room on the mezzanine."[21]

Now, you obviously feel some pressure to come back and not to go to the Valencia Room. But you do have a choice. And while there is pressure, you are not being forced back. Bethune can underscore that you did have choice if, at 1:30, he says, "As I said before lunch, it is your choice to be back here this afternoon." Faced with the fact that you have chosen irrevocably and publicly to show up after lunch for more pain and sacrifice, you have to explain why you did it. Now you are more receptive to justifications such as "I will learn a lot from this," "This gives me some great contacts," "These ideas could affect the whole industry," and "This is a firm on the move." You persuade yourself using these new, culturally accepted reasons simply because now it's easier to change your beliefs than it is to change your action. Your action of returning has already taken place. Others have seen you return and sit down. Thus it's harder to change that action ("Whoops, got into the wrong room") than it is to change your beliefs, especially when there are supportive beliefs at hand.

This is cultural change writ small. But it is also cultural change writ deep.

The Content of Culture

So far we have presented a general picture of organizational culture by suggesting several dimensions that have been used to describe it. Culture is about sufficient, but not excessive, similarity of approach and priorities. We referred to this as loosely coupled sharing to highlight the fact that culture is never monolithic. If you want to get a feel for the culture of a place, you need to see what people expect, what values and beliefs they share, what assumptions they feel are essential to successful coping, and how they do things locally. These are all issues of form. The *content* of culture refers to something different. Content is about the specifics that are loosely shared: the specific approaches, priorities, assumptions, expectations, values, and practices that bind people. When people say, for instance, culture is "how we do things around here," what exact "things" do they have in mind? And what are the boundaries of "around here," and what would be placed outside those boundaries, as "over there"?

In looking at content more closely, we will use as our example the influential notion of an "informed culture." An informed culture is a good illustration of a mindful culture. An informed culture is also a cornerstone of so-called safety cultures, and it is an important analytical framework that imposes order on chaotic events such as those associated with the Bristol Royal Infirmary.

The common content thread in cultures that strive to be mindful, informed, and safe is that they all focus on wariness. They try to "anticipate the worst and equip themselves to deal with it at all levels of the organization." (Recall the first principle, "preoccupation with failure.") "It is hard, even unnatural, for individuals to remain chronically uneasy, so their organizational culture takes on a profound significance. Individuals may forget to be afraid, but the culture of a high reliability organization provides them with both the reminders and the tools to help them remember."[22]

If people grow complacent and forget to be afraid, one way to instill wariness is to gather the right kinds of information. An informed culture is "one in which those who manage and operate the system have current knowledge about the human, technical, organizational, and environmental factors that determine the safety of the system as a whole."[23] James Reason worries most about events and entities that penetrate and breach an organization's defenses, so he pays close attention to whether a safety culture creates and sustains intelligent wariness. His data suggest that the best way to maintain these states of wariness is to collect and disseminate information about incidents, near misses, and the state of the system's vital signs.

The problem is that candid reporting of errors takes trust and trustworthiness. Both are hard to develop, easy to destroy, and hard to institutionalize. Reason argues that it takes four subcultures to ensure an informed culture. Assumptions, values, and artifacts must line up consistently around

1. Reporting culture—what gets reported when people make errors or experience near misses

2. Just culture—how people apportion blame when something goes wrong

3. Flexible culture—how readily people can adapt to sudden and radical increments in pressure, pacing, and intensity

4. Learning culture—how adequately people can convert the lessons that they have learned into reconfigurations of assumptions, frameworks, and action

All four are necessary for people to be informed and for safe operations. There were problems with all four subcultures at the Bristol Royal Infirmary. In the following analysis, we take special note of the ways in which a less informed culture produced less wariness and more fatalities. Keep in mind that less mindful practices associated with failure, simplification, operations, resilience, and expertise are at work in these tragic events.

The Bristol Royal Infirmary Case

This is a case involving children under the age of one year, with hearts no bigger than a walnut, undergoing complex open-heart surgery to correct one of twelve anomalies. Incidents at the Bristol Royal Infirmary (BRI) are noteworthy because in five of the seven years between 1988 and 1994, the BRI mortality rate for open-heart surgery in children under age one year was roughly double that of other centers in England.[24] A board of inquiry was convened to investigate this pattern. The board concluded that the Pediatric Cardiac Service (PCS)

> was less than adequate over the whole period of our Terms of reference and as regards open-heart surgery on all children, whether under or over 1. But this judgment, to the extent that it is based on reliable and verifiable evidence, relies heavily on hindsight. At the time, while the PCS service was less than adequate, *it would have taken a different mindset from the one which prevailed* on the part of the clinicians at the center of the service and senior management to come to this view. It would have required abandoning the principles

which then prevailed, of optimism, of learning curves, and of gradual improvements over time, and adopting what may be called the precautionary principle. This did not occur to them. This is one of the tragedies of Bristol.[25]

To focus, as the investigation board did, on the importance of a "different mindset" is to link the BRI experience with the culture that shapes and sustains what people know (informed culture) and how they go about knowing it (mindfulness). Since a mind-set reflects a prevailing culture, we need to fill in a bit more background before taking a closer look at BRI's culture.

The Bristol Royal Infirmary and the Bristol Royal Hospital for Sick Children, also known as Bristol Children's Hospital (BCH), are teaching hospitals associated with Bristol University's Medical School located in southwestern England.[26] In 1984, BRI was designated by the National Health Service (NHS) as a center to provide open-heart surgery, and the BCH was designated to provide closed-heart surgery. The NHS assumed that "[a] unit should undertake a certain volume of cases to ensure good results in this very exacting field." The idea was that the more the practice, the better a center would become, and the more likely it would be to experience over time a complete range of rare conditions and complications.[27]

The regional health authority and hospital board at Bristol relied on the CEO, Dr. John Roylance, for direction of the hospitals and surgical units. Roylance in turn relied on Dr. James Wisheart, one of the two pediatric surgeons who operated on babies. Wisheart was a man of all trades, holding other positions in BRI such as associate director of cardiac surgery and chair of the hospital's medical committee. The other pediatric surgeon was Dr. Janardan Dhasmana. Wisheart and Dhasmana operated on both children and adults. But pediatric cardiac surgery was only a small part of the overall cardiac surgery activity. Experts agreed that the minimum annual caseload necessary for a center to maintain sufficient expertise was approximately eighty to one hundred open-heart operations for two surgeons (forty to fifty per surgeon per year).[28] The Bristol open-heart pediatric caseload for children under one year of age was low, averaging about forty-six between the two surgeons.

When the pediatric cardiac surgical program began, its performance was roughly commensurate with the other eleven programs in the Health Service, but over the next seven years, while all other centers improved their performance, Bristol did not. As events unfolded over the years, there were at least 101 formal "concerns" raised about the quality of care being delivered, including those raised by Dr. Stephen Bolsin, a consultant anesthetist who joined BRI in 1988. Bolsin immediately noted differences between his previous experience at Brompton Hospital and his experience at BRI. In contrast to Brompton, surgeries at BRI lasted longer, which meant that the babies were being kept on the bypass machines much longer, with more severe adverse results. In 1995, the deaths of several children brought events to a crescendo, and the surgeries were halted. Parents called for an inquiry in 1996. The inquiry started on June 18, 1998, and ended with the publication of the report in July 2001. The board heard from 577 witnesses, including 238 parents; studied nine hundred thousand pages of documents; examined eighteen hundred medical records; took oral evidence for ninety-six days; and commissioned 180 papers submitted to seven seminars.[29] In separate actions, the medical licenses of Drs. Roylance and Wisheart were revoked, and Dr. Dhasmana was not allowed to do surgery on children for three years.[30]

Culture comes into play at BRI because in its final report, the board of inquiry variously referred to BRI as a provider-oriented culture, a culture of blame, a club culture where one's career depends on whether one fit into the inner circle and not on one's performance, a culture of fear, an oral culture, a culture of justification, a culture of paternalism ("Professionals know best, so don't ask questions"), and a culture of uncertainty.[31] While this list has the ring of a concept run amok, what it does suggest is that there exist at BRI cultural differentiation, fragmentation, and diverse expectations regarding what is appropriate. Thus within the BRI system, people expect that the needs of providers will be honored, that blame will be shifted away from individuals, that seniority will determine who makes decisions, that speaking up depends on where you are in the hierarchy, that nothing gets written down, that justifications protect providers, that questions are out of place, and that uncertainty is dismissed rather than dealt with. Common to these several "cultures" is the fact that they are closed to revision, failure-averse, and focused on uncertainty reduction through justification of current outcomes. In the vocabulary of our book, the inquiry board's snapshot of the various BRI cultures suggests mindless practices with minimal interest in questions, feedback, and inquiry. The result is that system flaws go unnoticed. And because they are unnoticed, they incubate and enlarge and are neither anticipated nor contained. The question at BRI was, are our practices "less than ideal," or are they "unacceptably poor"?[32] "Less than ideal" implies that professionals need to learn more. "Unacceptably poor" implies that the surgeons should pull the plug, stop operating, and send patients elsewhere. Cultures at BRI favored the first interpretation and discouraged the second one.

BRI and Informed Culture

We further organize the portrait of cultures at BRI by briefly sampling indications that BRI was not an "informed culture." We examine the four subcultures that James Reason identified: reporting, just, flexible, and learning.

Reporting Culture. Since safety cultures are dependent on the knowledge gained from rare incidents, mistakes, near misses, and other "free lessons," they need to be structured so that people feel willing to discuss their own errors. A reporting culture is about protection of people who report (this is also a provision of a just culture). It is also about what kinds of reports are trusted. As events unfolded, people at BRI could have been more alert to unexpected events so that they could anticipate them, avoid them, and mitigate their effects. Without knowing what is going on, you have no idea how safe it is for the patient to be there, no idea how to take corrective action, no learning, and a high risk that it will happen again.

There are several features of the reporting culture at BRI that drastically curbed the dissemination of reports about errors and possible corrections. For example, BRI was described as an "oral culture" in which there was almost no written communication (no minutes taken of meetings, for example). This meant that if you were outside the circle that discussed anything, you didn't know what other people had experienced and learned.[33] This limitation was made worse because a small group of high-level personnel talked mostly to each other and constituted what was called a "club culture." For example, Drs. Wisheart and Roylance had been schoolmates and had known each other for thirty years. They were the center of the "club." To challenge the performance of those in the club meant that you were being disloyal, which moved you outside the inner circle and meant that your information was severely limited. The anesthetist, Dr. Stephen Bolsin, spoke up repeatedly, but his concerns were dismissed because he was regarded as disloyal to the club and therefore an outsider.[34] Because reporting was considered evidence of disloyalty, the board concluded that "too few had too much power and were not open about work or colleagues."[35]

There were other problems with reporting, one of them being the physical layout of the cardiac services. Open-heart procedures were conducted at BRI, but cardiologists were located at Children's Hospital, and babies were transported back to wards at Children's, two blocks away, shortly after they had been stabilized. Separate sets of notes were kept at each site, and notes might not accompany the child during the move to the other site.[36] To make matters worse, the nursing staffs for the intensive care units (ICUs) at the two sites were feuding over turf, and the closed-heart nurses had more experience, which they were unwilling to share.[37] Reporting and dissemination were also curtailed because surgeons used their own personal "logs of operations" as the primary sources of data on how they were doing. They perceived in those logs a pattern of complex cases and concluded that their poor results happened because they were "caring for an unusually high proportion of unusually difficult cases."[38]

From these and other examples of a flawed reporting culture,[39] it is clear that BRI had poor-quality information to work with. And what information it had was restricted in its dissemination. Furthermore, we see a remarkable lack of mindfulness in just these reporting practices. All five principles of high reliability are violated: failures are not made salient, deaths are simplistically labeled anomalies, procedures are not tight, recoveries from deteriorating conditions are missing, and there are no experts in the system to defer to.

Just Culture. The BRI board of inquiry was mindful of a just culture when it said, "A culture of safety crucially requires the creation of an open, free, non-punitive environment in which healthcare professionals can feel safe to report adverse events and near misses."[40] We have already seen that BRI's informed culture was not open and free, nor was it regarded as nonpunitive. But the notion of a just culture highlights an additional property of being informed.

An organization is defined by how it handles blame and punishment, and that, in turn, can affect what gets reported in the first place. A just culture is described as "an atmosphere of trust in which people are encouraged, even rewarded, for providing essential safety-related information—but in which they are clear about where the line must be drawn between acceptable and unacceptable behavior."[41] That line is crucial because it separates unacceptable behavior that deserves disciplinary action from acceptable behavior for which punishment is not appropriate and the potential for learning is considerable. It is impossible to do away with such a line altogether because "a culture in which all acts are immune from punishment would lack credibility in the eyes of the workforce."[42] Reason reports that when this line is clear, only about 10 percent of the unsafe acts actually fall into the "unacceptable" category.[43] This means that the other 90 percent are blameless and could be reported without fear of punishment. But if people are unclear about what constitutes grounds for punishment, if people feel ashamed to admit errors, and if management deals with errors in an inconsistent manner, that 90 percent will be concealed. As a result, the system will be seriously deficient in understanding how vulnerable it really is.

We see lapses in a just culture at BRI around fears that informal internal audits of clinical practice and outcomes will get into management hands. "Anxious to allay fears that information could fall into the hands of management (a prospect which, at the time, was judged by many professionals to be unacceptable), the process of medical audit was insulated from management and put under the direction of doctors. Audit was represented as an educational tool, not a mechanism for accountability."[44]

We also see lapses in a just culture in the way investigations of adverse events were handled by the regional health system. These inquiries, which were conducted in a "prevailing culture of blame and stigma," tended to single out "an individual or group who are held to have been responsible. The individual is condemned . . . [and] the matter is resolved: until the next serious failure."[45] The board report then pointed to the obvious flaw in this approach to justice:

> While it may be appropriate to criticise some individual(s), it is often too easy a response to stop at this point. Crucially, it deflects attention from the context in which that individual was working. The individual may be replaced, but the underlying environment, which gave rise to the problem, goes on. It will only be a matter of time, therefore, before the same, or similar, set of problems arise again in the same place or elsewhere.[46]

To be mindful is to resist the powerful temptation to blame individuals. Practices of blaming create an atmosphere that tends to stigmatize people and discourage them from speaking up. People who speak up on behalf of the *system* can avoid such stigma, but only if the culture rewards practices that are preoccupied with *system* failure. This is tough to do, as Diane Vaughan makes clear:

> Invariably, the politics of blame directs our attention to certain individuals and not others when organizations have failures. Invariably, the accepted explanation is some form of "operator error," isolating in the media spotlight someone responsible for the hands-on work: the captain of the ship, a political functionary, a technician, or middle-level managers. To a great extent, we are unwilling participants because without extraordinary expenditure of time and energy we cannot get beyond appearances. But we are also complicitous, for we bring to our interpretation of public failures a wish to blame, a penchant for psychological explanations, an inability to identify the structural and cultural causes, and a need for a straightforward, simple answer that can be quickly grasped. But the answer is seldom simple.[47]

Flexible Culture. A flexible culture is one that adapts to changing demands. James Reason equates flexibility with the shifting authority structures that we discussed as the fifth process of mindfulness, deference to expertise. The key assumption behind the call for a flexible culture is that information tends to flow more freely when hierarchies are flattened and rank defers to technical expertise. Thus flexibility and deference go hand in hand. The important anchor in any discussion of flexibility is a finding that was central in the board of inquiry's thinking about BRI. Centers for cardiac surgery that had a lower mortality rate than BRI "had a *better record of rescue* of the complications [that developed], that is, they recognized them earlier and treated them better, for the same severity score."[48] This finding underscores the importance of the HRO principle of commitment to resilience, and it suggests the kind of flexible culture that Reason seems to have in mind.

We have already suggested that expectations at BRI reflected a rigid rather than flexible culture. But there was an odd form of flexibility at work at BRI. You will recall that BRI did not have a dedicated pediatric cardiac surgeon. Instead, it had been searching for one off and on for years, and medical personnel saw themselves as making do until the position was filled (it was filled in 1995). They called this approach "make do and mend."[49] Noble as this may sound, it is an invitation to disaster. In the words of the inquiry board, "Such an approach is ultimately hopeless. It exploits the preparedness of the professionals to sacrifice themselves while exhausting them. As a recipe for the future it is useless." It is also potentially useless because, again, it places responsibility for flexibility in the hands of individuals rather than systems.

There was additional inflexibility in the way ward rounds were conducted in the ICUs. In postoperative management of patients, the anesthetists and surgeons carried out separate ward rounds. "As a consequence, nursing staff felt that they received conflicting instructions. A course of action indicated by one clinician might be changed by another on a later ward round."[50] This rigid practice of separate rounds continued without change because of boundaries between specialties. The practice often led to the undoing of complex treatment plans already set in motion by professionals who had seen the baby earlier. Since communications among specialties were minimal, conflicts in treatment plans tended to persist longer than was appropriate. Remember, the patients are very young babies whose conditions can change much more rapidly than is true for adult patients.

Smooth patient transfers among services require flexibility, teamwork, and information, but all three were problematic, as we have seen:

> A number of parents described to us their confusion and distress at having to move from one hospital to the other, particularly when they feared that the move was not well planned and prepared. Michelle Cummings told us that on moving her daughter, Charlotte, back to the [Children's Hospital] after surgery at the BRI: "... They didn't even know we were coming. . . . There was no intensive

bed for her, no life support machine, and they were still hand venti-lating her." Charlotte's medical notes state that she was: "Transferred from Ward 5. Arrived unannounced as usual."[51]

Learning Culture. If timely and candid information generated by knowledgeable people is available and disseminated, an informed culture can become a learning culture.[52] The combination of candid reporting, justice, and flexibility enable people to witness best prac-tices that occur within their own boundaries and to move toward adoption of them. An informed culture learns by means of ongoing debates about constantly shifting discrepancies. These debates pro-mote learning because they identify new sources of hazard and dan-ger and new ways to cope.

Learning was not prevalent at BRI. Sentences like the follow-ing show up over and over in the BRI inquiry report: "They were too easily persuaded that their poor results were a run of bad luck or that things would improve."[53] One of the consultants to the inves-tigating board, Professor Marc de Laval, articulated what would have been a better learning subculture at BRI:

> "While regretting them, we must all learn 'to treasure mistakes,' be-cause of what they can teach us for the future. This calls for an ex-tremely mature organisation and equally, a mature society. It means an abandonment of the easy language of blame in favour of a com-mitment to understand and learn. It calls for significant leadership. It calls for practical action geared to be more open about error and mistakes."[54]

Opportunities for learning at BRI were often overlooked. When patients expressed "concerns," which normally would be occasions for learning, the concerns were labeled "complaints," and actions were taken to neutralize or defend against them rather than to seek direct feedback in order to improve.[55] Consistent with this defen-sive stance, personnel waited for complaints to be made and did not actively seek feedback.[56] Even though it is the duty of clinicians at

BRI "to challenge their own rather easy explanations," this didn't happen.[57]

There were moments of learning at BRI even though cultural supports for doing so were minimal. For example, operations involving the arterial switch procedure were halted in September 1992 after the deaths of five babies. On December 1, Dr. Dhasmana visited a pediatric cardiac surgeon at Birmingham Children's Hospital, where he talked about the procedure, observed an operation, and took a videotape of the operation home with him for reference.[58] In July, Dhasmana returned to Birmingham for further training. Upon completion of the training, he decided to stop doing the arterial switch procedure because he still could not transfer the adult procedure to neonates.[59] Although this episode could have served as a model for other personnel, it wasn't, because learning and the practices that produce it were not valued. They were not valued because the prevailing attribution was that adverse outcomes were due to unduly complex cases, not to inadequacies that could be remedied by learning and information sharing.

As a final complication in creating and sustaining a learning culture, there is a troublesome problem that is tied up with litigation. Obvious cases of error tend to be settled out of court, and there is no public discussion of the issues involved. Hence little can be learned from these cases. The cases that are not settled and that do go to trial and become publicly known tend to be *borderline* cases in which it is less clear that a hospital or professional were at fault. These public cases are the "noisy" settings from which it is much more difficult to extract lessons. Thus the worst cases that could provide the best learning generate the least amount of learning[60] and are most likely to happen again.

BRI and You

There were so many departures from safety, mindfulness, and an informed culture at BRI that the preceding discussion might seem a bit like "shooting fish in a barrel." The BRI system was so obviously flawed that it hardly seems worthwhile to pause over its problems.

But if the flaws are obvious to us, why weren't they obvious to the people involved? Would you have done any better in a culture that preferred that you work in the dark unless you were the "top dog"? Would you have realized the extent of your incompetence if you had been keeping score on your own performance? Would you have been any more successful speaking up when no one else in the system seemed to be listening? Could you have resisted the seductive explanation that babies were dying because they were complex cases and not because you had insufficient skills to repair their hearts? And could you, with vague data, have avoided the explanation that you were *gradually* getting better and would be getting better even faster if the nursing staff were more skilled? Probably not.

Culture is an invisible hand, but it is also a heavy hand. Norms that control "what we do around here" and "what we expect around here" are binding on people because they want to belong to groups of similar specialists and want to be esteemed by those specialists. If you look back at Edgar Schein's definition of culture mentioned earlier in this chapter, what is striking is that it is anchored in adaptation and learning. But it doesn't pin down the specifics of that adaptation. Culture is built around practices that work. Even if those practices work in ways that outsiders abhor, those practices still hold some systems together. And that's why they are tough to change. BRI learned to cope with its external and internal problems by rationalizing its work as focused on unusually complex cases, a conclusion that was sustained by weak mindfulness, limited information, and concentrated power.

Chapter Summary

The message of this chapter is that mindfulness must be treated as a culture as well as a set of principles that guide practice. Culture is a pattern of shared beliefs and expectations, along with a repertoire of capacities for action, which shape how individuals and groups detect, manage, and learn from the unexpected. Culture produces a sufficient similarity of approach, outlook, and priorities that people are able to enact collective, sustained responses. Culture exerts centralized control over dispersed activities by means of a handful of core values that are credibly enacted by top management, widely accepted by people in the organization, and used continuously to interpret and express appropriate behaviors. To sustain mindful management of the unexpected, you need to weave principles of mindfulness into values, expectations, and norms that support local practices.

Culture change involves modifying practices, artifacts, values, and assumptions, usually tackling those four properties in that order under the assumption that people act their way into new beliefs and values. Change toward greater mindfulness often involves movement toward a more informed culture that is focused on reporting, justice, flexibility, and learning. We used James Reason's ideas of an informed culture to show how inattention to mindfulness contributed to excess deaths at the Bristol Royal Infirmary and how more reliance on mindful processes might have forestalled the tragedy. We saw that more openness and less blaming lead people to ask "What happened?" and not "Who is at fault?"

In Chapter Seven, we shift the focus from culture back to the individual and propose several guidelines for incorporating principles of anticipation and containment into local practices that are meaningful for you.

7

How to Manage Mindfully

If you want to generate action that is more reliable, resilient, and mindful, then you need to make the five principles involving failures, simplification, operations, resilience, and expertise a higher priority. In this chapter, we focus on several small, cumulative changes that help you add mindfulness to your current practices. These small changes are things you can build into your managerial style to better manage the unexpected. We have set the chapter up this way because we know that you can't just shut your organization down while you figure out ways to make it more reliable and resilient. Instead, you have to develop more mindful ways of organizing while still doing what people expect you to do. That's tough because you have to keep making sense of current demands using your old frameworks while you simultaneously raise questions about whether those frameworks are still as useful as they used to be.[1]

A change strategy built around consistent, incremental small changes that produce visible results has been called a *small wins strategy*. Formally, a small win is a "concrete, complete, implemented outcome of moderate importance."[2] Small wins produce change without confronting the system directly or aggressively. They also test implicit theories about resistance and opportunities within the firm, promote learning, and often lower resistance to subsequent proposals.

Organizational change involving small wins should not be confused with the idea that one way to accomplish a big task is to break it down into several small steps that are accomplished one by one. Small wins, instead, are opportunistic steps that move in the same general direction but often are noteworthy because they move away from bad conditions. They are not necessarily logical, sequential steps that lead steadily to a clear goal. Success using that kind of progression requires a stable environment, and that's not what HROs face. Furthermore, small wins often uncover achievable goals that were not envisioned before wins began to accumulate. Small wins are controllable in the sense that they depend mostly on your own actions. Small wins have their impact through the tangible examples they provide for others, through the allies they attract and the opponents they deter, through doing something tangible, and through creating a context within which change is now seen as possible. A manager attuned to small wins is a person who is attentive to things like questions that are frequently or never asked, what's first and last on a meeting agenda, what is and isn't important enough to call a meeting, and what gets followed up and what gets forgotten. Each of these are viewed as "sites" where the ways in which people handle failures, simplifications, operations, resilience, and expertise can be altered.

Before we examine how small improvements can get started, let's take a second look at wildland fire management, this time noting ways in which fire managers are moving toward more mindful practices. These changes may suggest newer ways of working that you might try. Our intention in this chapter is to describe both wildland firefighting initiatives and other kinds of initiatives that, taken together, can lead to greater success in managing the unexpected. And we want these descriptions to be on a scale that you can introduce without waiting around until someone higher up "gets it."

First, the firefighters.

Mindfulness in Wildland Firefighting

During the year 2000 fire season, when the Cerro Grande prescribed fire escaped, the combined agencies that manage wildland fire lit 4,697 prescribed fires that cleared 1,192,220 acres of land. By the end of 2005, those numbers had increased to 7,756 prescribed fires that cleared 2,310,346 acres.[3] As prescribed fires have increased in number and complexity, there have also been modest changes toward more mindful managing of wildfire. During that time, agencies have spent funds to buy more equipment, hire and train more people, and update both computer systems and fire behavior models. In other words, agencies have used their funds to do basically the same things they've been doing all along. These are the easy changes to make. It is easier to buy stuff than it is to create and stabilize new ways of relating, new frameworks for organizing, and new expectations and norms. Those are the tough, messy issues that accompany shifts to more mindful, reliable, resilient functioning. Although ambitious purchasing may look like a preoccupation with failure and greater sensitivity to operations, it basically involves the continued application of old categories with little refinement. It is business as usual, albeit in a far more hostile environment.

But there are outcroppings of mindful organizing that are beginning to take hold and diffuse in wildland firefighting. These changes illustrate that practices can be designed to implement the five principles. Consider a simple example. Firefighters are admonished to follow "the Ten Standard Fire Orders."[4] Whenever an adverse incident occurs, one of the first questions asked is, "Were all ten orders followed?" This question is not as straightforward as it sounds. Several experienced firefighters contend that it is impossible to follow all ten orders while fighting fire.[5] Part of the problem is that the orders have been simplified since they were first drafted in 1957. Karl Brauneis has resisted this simplification and has restored the original intent of these orders by structuring a rewrite so that you move step by step from order 1 to order 10 to *engage* the fire and step by step from order 10 to order 1 when you *disengage* from the fire.[6] Each order builds on the one before it. The small win here is that a previous assortment of simplified orders has been converted into an orderly process that is more nuanced (HRO Principle 2). Guidelines that firefighters know well have been preserved but made more mindful through reordering and refinement. A related change in the orders has been made by the National Wildfire Coordinating Group (NWCG), which has grouped the orders into three clusters: fire behavior, fireline safety, and organizational control.[7]

A different form of attention to mindfulness is found in modifications to interagency relationships so that sensitivity to operations and resilience is increased. For example, since the 2000 Cerro Grande fire, Bandelier Superintendent Darlene M. Koontz and other fire management personnel have worked actively to build a network of relationships among fire agencies, the local communities such as Los Alamos and Santa Fe, and other regional stakeholders.[8] If you put on your mindfulness hat, you see that these efforts assemble and direct a more diverse set of perspectives at an increasingly complex environment. When you think in terms of mindfulness, you see that agencies that act like silos are a form of simplification and that creating a network of relationships is a tangible way to decrease silos and increase requisite variety. A more complex set of interagency sensors is a better match for complex unexpected deviations. This is the same strategy that was used to mitigate adverse events at Diablo Canyon.

It is this network of relationships taken together—not necessarily any one individual or organization in the group—that can also maintain the big picture of operations during larger prescribed burns. The intense efforts since Cerro Grande to rebuild Bandelier's fire program and reestablish trust among the various regional stakeholders is finally paying off. Prescribed burning in the region had not been allowed since Cerro Grande. But after an extensive outreach program and frequent public meetings to share key lessons learned between Bandelier staff and the Los Alamos community, the Los Alamos city council passed a resolution in the summer of 2005 supporting Bandelier National Monument's resumption of prescribed burning.

Mindful firefighting is also being encouraged by means of a growing number of case studies, staff rides, practices, and research studies that show what it means to act more mindfully. Consider the case study involving how managers dealt with the Hawkins wildfire in the Dixie National Forest.[9] This fire burned over 35,000 acres and threatened the town of Enterprise in southern Utah. When a series of lightning strikes started several small wildland fires in late July 2004, twelve miles southwest of Enterprise, fire managers decided to "let the fires go." Fire agencies and local ranchers had been meeting for over a year to discuss concerns about the area's overgrown vegetation and had agreed to conduct a prescribed burn. Before fire managers could light the planned fire, nature did it for them. As Dixie National Forest Fire Management Officer Brett Fay recalls, "We *expected* the fire would burn around seven thousand acres; we didn't *expect* it would get so big." They also didn't expect that the fire would uncharacteristically change direction multiple times, grow so fast, cross a dirt road boundary, or generate so much smoke that the town's residents would need to be evacuated. Nor did they expect that the water source they had counted on would be unavailable.

Surprises kept cropping up, but every time a new surprise surfaced, managers updated their understanding of events. They weren't afraid to ask for help or admit they were in trouble. As a result, on the third fire day, after 12,500 acres had burned, the Hawkins fire was declared a wildfire to be suppressed. After the decision was made, Patti Koppenol, Intermountain Regions deputy regional fire director, claims she "heard a collective sigh of relief as people thought we had finally come to our senses."

The small win here, as in other case studies, is that people have a tangible example of what mindful work looks and feels like. They can ask questions such, "If I had been in Brett Fay's shoes, what would I have done, and what could I have done?" The case study becomes part of one's experience even if that experience is secondhand.

A different form of indirect, vicarious experience that qualifies as a small win is participation in a staff ride. The NWCG Wildland Fire Leadership Development Program, along with retired fire behavior specialist Dave Thomas, has championed staff rides. You may recall that the Cerro Grande incident that was reviewed in Chapter One was informed by a staff ride. Founders of the fire leadership development program have described staff rides this way:

> A staff ride is a case study that is conducted on the ground where the event happened. . . . The intent of a staff ride is to put participants in the shoes of the decision makers on a historical incident in order to learn for the future. A staff ride should not be a tactical-fault finding exercise. Participants should be challenged to push past the basic question of "What happened?" and examine the deeper questions of leadership and decision making: "What would I have done in this person's place?" "How detailed should the guidance from a superior to a subordinate be?" "Can a senior leader make use of a competent but overzealous subordinate?" "What explains repeated organizational success or failure?" The study of leadership aspects in a staff ride transcends time and place.[10]

Increasingly, staff rides are using the five HRO principles as a lens to interpret what happened. You, too, could take your team to the actual site where an unexpected event was handled either well or poorly, walk everyone through the decision making that was involved, and reflect on how to handle that event more mindfully.

As a final example of small wins in the pursuit of more mindful firefighting, we should mention the increased use of systematic procedures to review incidents and extract lessons. The best known of these procedures is the so-called after action review (AAR), built around four questions:

1. What did we set out to do?
2. What actually happened?
3. Why did it happen?
4. What are we going to do next time?[11]

Personnel at the Wildland Fire Lessons Learned Center, an interagency wildland fire resource center, have been concerned with the dissemination of the lessons learned from an AAR and have proposed a different set of four questions to share local learning more widely. They call these four questions an "AAR rollup":

1. What was the most notable success at the incident that others may learn from?

2. What were some of the most difficult challenges faced, and how were they overcome?

3. What changes, additions, or deletions are recommended to wildland fire training curriculums?

4. What issues were not resolved to your satisfaction and need further review? Based on what was learned, what is your recommendation for resolution?[12]

And one of the most striking recent examples of experimentation involving ways to encourage mindfulness is the peer review,[13] as exemplified by the "Peer Review Report of Balls Canyon Near-Miss, June 27, 2006."[14] The incident involved a three-person crew on an engine that got stuck while it was backing away from an exploding fire. The crew was rescued by a service truck just as fire engulfed the engine. This report, written in the form of a story, is built around a preoccupation with failure and uncovers "faint signals of error and mistakes" that could have led to catastrophic outcomes. The report is noteworthy because it attempts to bridge AARs and more formal investigations. The following questions were asked of the people involved in the Balls Canyon incident:

1. What was planned?

   a. What was your leader's intent?

   b. What information were you provided?

   c. What did you feel was missing?

   d. Why couldn't you get it?

2. What was the situation?

   a. What did you see?

   b. What were you aware you couldn't see?

3. What did you do?

   a. Why did you do it?

   b. What didn't you do?

   c. Why didn't you do it?

4. What did you learn?

   a. What might you do differently the next time?

   b. What can we learn as an organization?

All three sets of questions tap the extent to which people had a *rich awareness of discriminatory detail*, which details they saw and missed, and how attention and action could be deployed differently next time. These protocols are small wins because they trigger reflection that may lead to more mindful firefighting. You can ask these same questions to pinpoint where and how mindfulness could be improved in your own group. The questions are not intrusive, but they do presume that a just culture is in place and that candor won't be punished.

Even though bits and pieces of mindfulness are already evident, the fire community does not yet have a culture that binds those pieces together, animates them, institutionalizes them, and makes them prominent, consistent, and credible from top to bottom. This is still the case even though the goal of creating a self-learning and self-correcting culture to improve wildland firefighter safety has preoccupied wildland firefighting organizations for almost a decade.[15] For example, in a 1998 report on wildland firefighter safety awareness, we find the following comment about "transforming culture":

> The *culture change* process is a two-sided coin. On one side is the "bottom-up" phenomenon that many changes arise from those actually doing the work. On the other side is the "top-down" reality

that changes in conducting business often get made by direction or
sanction from top management. Both are essential. . . . Changing
the organizational culture . . . will require commitment at every organizational level. . . . Cultural change is not triggered by a magic
bullet or a directive. Rather, culture is changed by a series of small
steps taken by the leading members of the culture at all levels. Leadership is standing up and leading the way. It is behavior and it is
demonstrable. It is showing, not telling. . . . Changing the way business is conducted requires people at all levels to lead by personal example in demonstrating new approaches to achieve safer [and more
reliable] operations. . . . [This requires that we] strengthen accountability at all levels of the organization—firefighters, Crew Supervisors, fire managers, and up.[16]

Further small steps that can lead to organizing that is more mindful
are described next.

Small Wins in Mindful Organizing

As wildland fire managers make clear, mindfulness is both a mind-
set and a style of managing. We want you to focus on your own style
of managing, since this is the most immediate, the most influential,
and the most controllable means to start managing the unexpected.
If you convert a mindfulness mind-set into a mindful style of managing, you don't have to wait for slow culture change to take hold.
Instead, people can see firsthand, in your actions, that mindfulness
is practical, doable, and makes a difference. That is a powerful lesson. It will encourage others to follow your lead and adopt some of
the tools you use to stay on top of the unexpected. And these immediate, influential changes in your style of managing are something that you control. That's why we focus on small wins that set
cumulative changes in motion.

In the remaining pages, we look at examples of small wins that
summarize key lessons learned from HROs. Although other practices are also relevant, we focus on those that show up repeatedly in

the best HROs and that relate directly to the five processes that create a mindful infrastructure. These lessons supplement and occasionally reemphasize the lessons and guidelines you have encountered throughout this book. We look first at a sample of small wins that underlie the general mind-set associated with mindful organizing. Then we give examples of small wins for each of the five principles. Mindful management for resilient performance starts with you. You know how it works. You know why it works. You know where it works. And now we explore how to make it work.

Small Wins in the Basics of Mindfulness

Mindful organizing involves thinking differently about success, simplification, strategy, plans, and authority. That difference is about seeing the ways in which these apparent hallmarks of successful organizing can keep you from early detection of the unexpected. Possible small wins that move people from less mindful to more mindful functioning start with basics such as the following:

- *Remember that mindfulness takes effort.* Mindfulness is difficult to create because you're asking people to act unnaturally. In the interest of more mindfulness, you're asking people to pay more attention to their failures than to their successes, forgo recipes and rules of thumb in favor of what amounts to reinventing the wheel every time they act, pay attention to tactics and nuts and bolts rather than strategies and grand visions, get better at being reactive rather than proactive, and acknowledge that someone else may know more than they do. That's a big order. People would prefer to pay more attention to success, recipes, strategies, initiatives, and status. As an intermediate step in moving toward greater mindfulness, try to increase the number of mindful moments in your unit. A mindful moment consists of a short interval, such as trying to solve a modest problem, when people agree to look at failures, assume nothing, look closely at the work involved in the problem, brainstorm a resilient response, and pinpoint the expert who can handle the problem rather than the person accountable for it.

• *Offer support to people who are making an effort to become more mindful*. To be mindful is often to discover that things are not as they seem and that there is much to learn. To be mindful is to become susceptible to learning anxiety. And anxious people need what Edgar Schein calls "psychological safety."[17] People who are made anxious by the prospect of learning need support, practice fields, positive role models, and a positive vision that they will be better off with culture change toward mindfulness. Give them that safety. And don't cave in to some kind of silly bravado that says that "the way we do things around here" is to "gut it out," "sink or swim," or "dive off the burning platform." If people had been mindful in the first place, they wouldn't need such last-ditch heroics. Moves toward mindfulness are tough. Don't hang back from helping people who are trying to make those moves. And don't be scared to ask for help yourself.

• *Frame mindfulness in novel ways*. AES, the global power company, says and does some strange things. And one of the most unusual is its insistence that "we try to reinvent the wheel every chance we get."[18] Think about it. Reinventing the wheel is supposed to be the last thing any of us would want to do. And yet each time you reinvent the wheel, you're a slightly different person from the last time you reinvented the wheel. And those intervening experiences may just enable you to see something in the reinvention that you missed every time before. To be more mindful is to see things you missed, details that foreshadow new consequences, unsuspected leverage points, unforeseen vulnerabilities, and sequences that can be rearranged. Mindfulness amounts to seeing old things in new ways, which is pretty much the challenge when you try to reinvent the wheel but with a new understanding of what *wheel* means.

• *Mitigate complacency*. One of the more vivid "truths" known to HROs is that the past settles its accounts when something unexpected begins to incubate. Recall crisis expert Pat Lagadec's point in Chapter One that unexpected events are brutal audits that test structures that have been developed before chaos arrives. Are you ready for a brutal audit of your capability to act mindfully? Is your group ready? People aren't ready if they don't know the costs of mindless action in a complex, unpredictable world. They aren't ready if they don't know that unexpected events incubate. And they aren't ready if they don't have deepening knowledge of and experience with their work. Complacency destroys. Don't let it get a foothold.

• *Remember that reliability is not bankable.* You never get reliability and resilience behind you. If there is one flaw with the phrase "high reliability organizations," it is that it's too static. You're better off if you think and act in terms of high reliability *organizing*. Systems, teams, groups, and the best-laid plans unravel. You have to keep redoing them.

• *Carry your expectations lightly.* Rigid, deeply held expectations create blind spots. A small win is to weaken expectations and increase confidence that people can handle whatever comes along. When weaker expectations are disconfirmed, the unanticipated will be less disruptive. But be aware that if expectations are held lightly, they will give less guidance, and this will impose greater demands on attention.

• *Balance centralization with decentralization.* In HROs, decentralization and centralization are held in critical balance, often by means of tight social coupling around a handful of core cultural values and looser coupling around the means by which these values are realized. Excess centralization can weaken local containment and local variation, whereas excess decentralization can weaken the comprehension of wider threats and the capacity to coordinate responses.

• *Let culture do the controlling.* A strong culture, held together by consistent values and enforced by social pressure, is all the control you need. Most managers overdo control. They heap hierarchy on top of rules on top of routines on top of job descriptions on top of culture and then wonder why people feel constrained and put forth less than their best efforts. Consensus plus intensity focused on a handful of values is a powerful guide. And a sufficient one. Be pragmatic in narrowing down to key values. Pose two questions: First, what do we do over and over that works well? If we keep doing that, it must be important. Second, what value is implied by those actions? Help people get comfortable asking and answering those questions. That is the beginning of acting your way into a new set of values.

Small Wins in the Development of a Preoccupation with Failure

Preoccupation with failure involves four questions:

1. What needs to go right?
2. What could go wrong?
3. How could things go wrong?
4. What things have gone wrong?

Answers often lie in small failures in the past that give clues to how the system might unravel again. If you are attentive to small failures, this does not mean that you're paralyzed by worries about screwing up. Instead it means you are actively searching for weak signals that the system is acting in unexpected ways. Small wins that move toward this mind-set include the following:

- *Restate your goals in the form of mistakes that must not occur.* Every strategy can be restated as mistakes to be avoided, threats to sidestep, bullets to dodge. Continental Airlines' strategy is to "fund the future," which can be restated as a mistake to avoid, namely, don't run out of cash. Similarly, "teamwork matters" means don't play favorites. "Act responsibly" means don't fudge test results to the Environmental Protection Agency. "Be informed" means don't let the ship run aground on your watch. Every strategy has a dark side. And mindful practices that put people on notice to look for failures help detect the onset of dark moments earlier, when a more decisive remedy is possible

- *Create awareness of vulnerability.* Get comfortable asking people, "What's risky around here?" Managers must sensitize employees to the possibility of unexpected errors that could escalate. People need to worry about vulnerability and feel accountable for reliability. Remember that awareness of vulnerability increases opportunities for learning. People need to be reminded that even though they think they understand their system and the ways in which it can fail, surprises are still possible. They have neither seen every possible failure mode nor imagined every one that is possible.

• *Create an error-friendly learning culture*. Work group learning improves when people seek feedback, share information, ask for help, talk about errors, and experiment. Be sure you create a climate of openness where people can engage in these behaviors and learn from errors.

• *Define the near miss*. Do you know what a near miss is in your organization, and do you talk about near misses when they occur? Do you interpret a near miss as a sign that your system's safeguards are working or as a sign that the system is vulnerable? Err on the side of danger. Interpret a near miss as danger in the guise of safety rather than safety in the guise of danger. Danger disguised as safety is a stronger sign of vulnerability than safety disguised as danger. Put discussions of near misses and their meaning on your agenda. Raise the comfort level in talking about them.

• *Clarify what constitutes good news*. Is no news good news, or is no news bad news? Don't let this remain a question. Remember, no news can mean either that things are going well or that someone is incapacitated and unable to give news, which is bad news. Don't fiddle with this one. No news is bad news. All news is good news, because it means that the system is responding. The good system talks incessantly. When it goes silent, that's unexpected, that's trouble, that's bad news.

Small Wins in the Development of Resistance to Simplification

"Keep it simple, stupid," is music to our ears. Simple rules of thumb are easy to remember, easy to practice, and easy to teach. Contingencies, nuance, differences, and details take more effort to retain but also better preserve weak signs of the unexpected. It takes complicated sensors to register complicated dynamic events. Small wins that move in this direction include the following:

- *Raise doubts to raise information*. Keep asking people, "Have you noticed anything out of the ordinary?" Praise them for an affirmative answer. And disseminate what they have spotted. What are people *not* seeing? Look for the inconceivable, because in doing so, you are trying to look outside the confines of your current expectations. Deny nothing. Try to see what your expectations keep you from seeing. It's easier to do this when you work with other people and alert them that this is precisely what you're trying to do.

- *Encourage alternative frames of reference*. Reward units that preserve divergent analytical perspectives. Members of groups tend not to share the unique knowledge they hold and prefer instead to talk mostly about information they all hold in common. Rely on exercises such as brainstorming or adversarial reviews that encourage people to raise questions and reveal information that is not widely shared. Divergent perspectives provide you with a broader set of assumptions and sensitivity to a greater variety of inputs. This discourages simplification and also increases the chance of seeing a greater number of problems in the making.

- *Put a premium on interpersonal skills*. Variety has a price: it can increase the incidence of disagreement and conflict when the time comes to act. Strengthen skills of conflict resolution and negotiation. Foster norms that encourage mutual respect for differences and discourage bullheadedness, hubris, headstrong acts, and self-importance. Develop organizational agreements about how to disagree constructively, propose rules for negotiating differences, and develop policies that reconcile organizational contradictions (for example, rewarding individuals while supporting the value of collaboration and cooperation).

- *Revise assessments as evidence changes*. De Keyser and Woods explain that when people get involved in unexpected events, they tend to hold on to their interpretation of the situation, an interpretation that was correct when first formed despite new evidence that the situation has changed or differs from their original assessment.[19] Even as opportunities to revise their interpretations occur, they are fixated on their original assessments of the situation and discount or rationalize away discrepant information.[20] Fresh eyes tend to break up the mind-set that perpetuates fixation. When people resist simplification, they tend to break up fixations. Your job is to be sure that people keep updating as evidence changes.[21]

- *Treat all unexpected events as information.* Use unexpected events as data points for learning, especially if they rarely occur. Be especially mindful of the temptation to redefine the unexpected as normal. That move conceals information and heightens risk. Treat small lapses as weak signals that *other* portions of the system may be at risk. Suspect that the causal chains that produced the unexpected event wind deep inside the system. Communicate information about weak signals widely.

- *Be mindful publicly.* Think out loud when you raise questions about categories, propose refinements, spot limitations, and see new features of context. When you inquire publicly, this helps people understand what is going on and provides a model for them to imitate. Overt displays of thought are a good thing. Overt displays of mindful thought are an even better thing.

Small Wins in the Development of Sensitivity to Operations

HROs are hands-on organizations, all the way up through the ranks. As a result, they are in close touch with what is going on. Operations are not delegated to some people while others think. Instead, HROs think while doing and by doing. That doing reflects their sensitivity to operations. Small wins that encourage, reward, and model a similar way of functioning include the following:

- *Reward contact with the front line.* Reward managers who stay close to the operating system or the frontline activities. Sensitivity to operations is a powerful means to keep up with developing situations. Managers who demonstrate ongoing attention to operations create a context where surprises are more likely to be surfaced and corrected before they grow into problems.

• *Speak up*. Just because you see something, don't assume that someone else sees it too. In a world of multiple realities and multiple expectations, one person's signal is another person's noise. Don't voluntarily withhold dissent. When you do, you reduce the system's ability to detect the unexpected. If people were scared to speak up to you, how would you know that? Ask them? Would they tell you? Be sure you model speaking up.

• *Develop skeptics*. Skepticism is a form of redundancy. When a report is met with skepticism and the skeptic makes an independent effort to confirm the report, there are now two observations where there was originally one. The second set of observations may support or refute the first set and may itself be double-checked by still another skeptic. Skepticism thus counteracts complacency and provides a more nuanced description of the context of operations that may in turn suggest more ways to deal with it.

• *Use rich media, and encourage people to listen*.[22] Face-to-face contact is perhaps the richest source of discriminatory detail because of the capacity for timely feedback, the ability to convey multiple cues, the degree to which the message can be personalized, the variety of language that can be used, and the range of meaning that can be conveyed. As richness is lost, so is key information. Richness declines as people move from face-to-face interaction to interaction by telephone, written personal communiqués (letters, memos, and e-mail), written formal communiqués (bulletins), down to the least rich source, numeric formal communiqués (printouts). Unexpected events are often confusing, and people need to use the richest possible media to build some idea of what they face. For example, debates about launching the *Challenger* spacecraft in unusually cold temperatures were conducted over a telephone, not face to face. With only voice cues, NASA did not have visual data such as facial expressions that might have given them fuller information about just how worried engineers were at the prospect of a launch.

• *Spend time on the front end of operations*. People need to know what they're doing and why they are doing it. Giving someone an order, by itself, is rarely a mindful practice because it lacks meaning. The small win that is implied here involves closer attention to how you brief people on forthcoming tasks. A useful starting point is a five-step briefing protocol that Gary Klein has labeled STICC (for *situation, task, intent, concern,* and *calibrate*).[23] When you brief people, spell out these five points:

1. *Situation:* Here's what I think we face.
2. *Task:* Here's what I think we should do.
3. *Intent:* Here's why I think that is what we should do.
4. *Concern:* Here's what we should keep our eye on because if that changes, we're in a whole new situation.
5. *Calibrate:* Now talk to me. Tell me if you don't understand, cannot do it, or see something I do not.

Once you pose a forthcoming situation in these terms, that situation is more meaningful. Equally important, it is now easier for people to spot the unexpected because they have a clearer idea of what to expect. Even though expectations are clearer, that does not mean you are more susceptible toward confirmation bias. The reason is step 4, concerns. In step 4, you say essentially, look, the situation may change, we may have to redo our expectations, watch out for that possibility. That is the epitome of sensitivity to operations.

Small Wins in the Development of a Commitment to Resilience

Life in HROs is a constant diet of interruptions and recoveries. Interruption is about stretching without collapsing. Recovering is about bouncing back from the stretch to something like what you started with. Resilience is important to both stages. Changes that improve resilience often look inefficient at the time. This means that your job is to encourage such 'inefficiencies," protect the people who produce them, and frame these inefficiencies as investments in resilience. Small wins that are consistent with these aims include the following:

- *Enlarge competencies and response repertoires.* Resilience takes deep knowledge. Generalized training and learning that increase people's response repertoires enlarge the range of issues that they notice and can deal with. So too, oddly enough, does a bad day when things go wrong. A bad day uncovers new details, evokes unpracticed responses, and provides a quiet lesson in the importance of persistence. All of these outcomes enlarge capabilities. When people enlarge their capability for action, they can see more hazards because whatever they see, they can now handle. Thus almost any growth in your group is a small win in the sense that it increases resilience. This phenomenon may be worth discussing and testing. Once a lesson is learned, ask people to record what looks different after the learning has occurred. Discuss those changes. Frame them as aids to recovery.
- *Don't overdo lean, mean ideals.* The lean, mean organization may sparkle in the short run, but it may also crash and burn at the first unexpected jolt because leanness strips the organization of resilience and flexibility. Realize that when managers eliminate "redundant" positions, they sacrifice experience and expertise. That loss can limit the repertoire of responses available to the organization. Improve resilience by forming knowledgeable people into ad hoc networks that self-organize to provide expert problem solving.
- *Accelerate feedback.* Effective resilience requires quick, accurate feedback so that the initial effects of attempted improvisations can be detected quickly and the action altered or abandoned if the effects are making things worse. Systems with slow feedback essentially give up any chance for resilience.
- *Treat your past experience with ambivalence.* When the unexpected deteriorates into a serious disruption, this result is an outcome that is partly novel and partly routine. You've seen lots of messes, but

you've never seen quite this particular mess. This means that your past experience is both partly relevant and partly irrelevant. Begin to contain the event by doing what experience tells you to do, but remain in doubt that you're doing exactly the right thing. Watch for what you have not seen before and deal with it immediately, but retain the context created by your past experience in the interest of keeping your intervention meaningful. You're simply engaging in simultaneous belief and doubt, admittedly a difficult exercise. Your goal is to act simultaneously as though the unexpected situation you face is just like every other situation you've faced and like no other situation you've ever faced.

Small Wins in the Development of Deference to Expertise

When people defer to expertise, this means that they are moving away from at least two assumptions: first, that authority equates to expertise, and second, that the higher one goes in a hierarchy, the greater the expertise. What people are moving toward are sites of expertise that are less obvious and more substantive. Small wins that are associated with expertise include the following:

• *Beware of the fallacy of centrality.* You need experts if you want to cope mindfully, but you need to be sure that your experts have a realistic view of their own expertise. If you defer to an expert who has limited self-awareness, you're in trouble. Here's why. Researcher Ron Westrum, observing the diagnostic practices of pediatricians in the 1940s and 1950s, spotted what he has come to call the fallacy of centrality.[24] The fallacy is this: under the assumption that you are in a central position, you presume that if something serious were happening, you would know about it. And since you don't know about it, it isn't happening. It is precisely this distortion that kept pediatricians from diagnosing child abuse until the early 1960s. Their reasoning? If parents were abusing their children, I'd know about it; since I don't know about it, it isn't happening.

When people are entrusted with dangerous technologies, it is easy for them to feel self-important and central since they live on a steady diet of people telling them that they are important. There is a grain of truth to these attributions. But that does not mean that these experts are also all-knowing. The problem can get even worse. If people assume you are all-knowing, they won't take the trouble to tell you what they know since they assume that you already know it. Recall how information may have been withheld from Paul Gleason at Cerro Grande in the belief that he already knew it. Gleason himself didn't commit the fallacy of centrality. But his associates, assuming that Gleason knew what they knew, failed to speak up and inform him. Hence Gleason didn't know that the fire was unusually volatile and had no reason to expect that this was the case. But he reached this conclusion not because of an inflated view of his own expertise but because his associates had an inflated view of his expertise and treated their own observations as redundant and therefore not worth expressing.

So listen more. Be wary of inflating your own expertise, and be wary of others who are similarly inclined. Self-important people know less than they think they do, are less curious about the world than they need to be, and are vulnerable to more surprises than they are prepared for. The mistaken claim that "nothing is happening" means simply that no one was looking or asking or listening.

• *Encourage imagination as a tool for managing the unexpected.* In Chapter Two, we mentioned that "imagination is not a gift usually associated with bureaucracies," but here we want to emphasize that it *is* a gift usually associated with the better HROs. Mindful management of the unexpected presumes that systems value expertise in imagination. Managing the unexpected consists of extrapolating the possible effects of small discrepancies, imagining scenarios not yet experienced, hypothetically constructing alternative lines of action, and envisioning what might have been overlooked given the narrow focus of a set of expectations. These are operations of imagination that can feel alien in cultures obsessed with measurement

and quantification. A small win would be to devote time in meetings to simulating alternative scenarios of anticipated futures and
working backward from an imagined outcome to identify the events
that could bring that outcome about. Alternatively, you can give
individuals or groups assignments to imagine scenarios of the unexpected and write them up.

- *Create flexible decision structures.* Don't assume that the expertise is at the top and disappears as you go down the hierarchy.
When problems occur, let decision making migrate to the people
who have the most expertise to deal with the problem. This means
that expertise and experience are more highly valued than rank
when unexpected situations arise.

Chapter Summary

Mindfulness is about the unexpected events that show up everywhere in corporate life (and everywhere else as well). Whether we
like it or not, if the world is filled with the unexpected, we're all firefighters putting out one fire after another. Most people resist that
depiction and like to lay claim to "loftier" activities, greater control,
and bolder initiatives. People want to get away from fighting fire so
they can get to the good stuff like planning, making strategy, and
forecasting. Those are supposed to be the high-prestige pastimes
where one finds the real action. The world of managing the unexpected through mindfulness suggests a different picture of prestigious action. As you implement the practices discussed throughout
this book, you'll discover that plans and forecasts can be inaccurate
and gain much of their clout from efforts to avoid information that
disconfirms them. You'll also discover that plans and forecasts create blind spots. Improvements in resilient performance lie in the
hands of those who have a deeper grasp of how things really work.
And that grasp comes in part from mindfulness. People who act
mindfully notice and pursue that rich, neglected remainder of information that less mindful actors leave unnoticed and untouched.
Mindful people hold complex projects together because they understand what is happening. That is what HROs can teach you.

Notes

Chapter 1: Managing the Unexpected

1. Pat Lagadec, *Preventing Chaos in a Crisis: Strategies for Prevention, Control, and Damage Limitation* (London: McGraw-Hill International, 1993), p. 54.
2. See Karl E. Weick, "The Collapse of Sensemaking in Organizations: The Mann Gulch Disaster," *Administrative Science Quarterly 38* (1993): 628–652.
3. National Park Service, *Cerro Grande Prescribed Fire Investigation Report, May 4–8, 2000* (Washington, D.C.: U.S. Department of the Interior, 2000), p. 11.
4. The burn boss is the person responsible to the agency administrator for implementing the prescribed fire plan.
5. Crucial to our analysis of the Cerro Grande incident is the interpretation that it is a system failure, not the failure of an individual. The distinction between a "person approach" and a "system approach" is common in the literature on errors and reliability. An example is James T. Reason, "Human Error: Models and Management," *British Medical Journal 220* (2000): 768–770.
6. Paul Shrivastava, *Bhopal: Anatomy of a Crisis*, 2nd ed. (London: Chapman, 1992).
7. Government Accountability Office, *Fire Management: Lessons Learned from the Cerro Grande (Los Alamos) Fire*, Document no. GAO/T-RCED-00-257 (Washington, D.C.: Government Accountability Office, July 20, 2000), p. 5.

8. National Park Service, *Cerro Grande Prescribed Fire, Board of Inquiry, Final Report* (Washington, D.C.: U.S. Department of the Interior, Feb. 26, 2001), p. 14.

9. David D. Woods and Erik Hollnagel, *Joint Cognitive Systems: Patterns in Cognitive Systems Engineering* (Boca Raton, Fla.: Taylor & Francis, 2006), pp. 69–96.

10. This scale is found in National Park Service, *Worksheet Numeric Rating Guide*, Document no. RM-18 (Washington, D.C.: U.S. Department of the Interior, 1998).

11. National Park Service, *Cerro Grande, Final Report*, pp. 14, 18.

12. Ibid., p. 22.

13. Ibid., p. 15.

14. Ibid., p. 16.

15. Ibid., p. 22.

16. Mica R. Endsley, "Toward a Theory of Situation Awareness in Dynamic Systems," *Human Factors* 37 (1995): 32–64. See also E. M. Roth, J. Multer, and T. Raslear, "Shared Situation Awareness as a Contributor to High Reliability Performance in Railroad Operations," *Organization Studies* 27 (2006): 967–987.

17. Government Accountability Office, "Fire Management," p. 6.

18. Author's notes on Paul Gleason, taped discussion of Cerro Grande, Santa Fe, N.M., May 12, 2004.

19. National Park Service, *Cerro Grande, Final Report*, p. 26.

20. Erik Hollnagel, "Resilience: The Challenge of the Unstable," in *Resilience Engineering: Concepts and Precepts*, ed. Erik Hollnagel, David D. Woods, and Nancy Leveson (Burlington, Vt.: Ashgate, 2006), p. 16.

21. The contrast between dealing with the unexpected by means of anticipation and dealing with the unexpected by means of resilience comes from Aaron Wildavsky, *Searching for Safety* (New Brunswick, N.J.: Transaction, 1991). Given the existence of unexpected risks, one has to choose between anticipation, which is understood as "sinking resources into specific defenses against particular anticipated risks," and resilience,

which is understood as "retaining resources in a form sufficiently flexible—storable, convertible, malleable—to cope
with whatever unanticipated harms might emerge" (p. 220).
As Wildavsky explains, "Where risks are highly predictable
and verifiable, and remedies are relatively safe, anticipation
makes sense; most vaccines fit this criterion of efficient anticipation. Where risks are highly uncertain and speculative,
and remedies do harm, however, resilience makes more sense
because we cannot know which possible risks will actually
become manifest" (p. 221). Our own personal bias, and the
tendency that we think we see in HROs, is to invest in knowledge and in command over resources in the belief that this will
enable us to mobilize a flexible response to the unexpected.
Thus we try to anticipate the unexpected, but we do so by
developing our capability for resilience. This means that we
maintain an ongoing commitment to improve self-knowledge,
relational knowledge, content knowledge, and capabilities to
act thinkingly.

22. Karl E. Weick, "Organizing and Failures of Imagination,"
    International Public Management Journal 8 (2005): 425–438.
23. Gary Klein, *Sources of Power: How People Make Decisions*
    (Cambridge, Mass.: MIT Press, 1998).
24. National Park Service, *Cerro Grande, Final Report*, p. 29.
25. Ibid., pp. 24–25.
26. Karlene H. Roberts, "Some Characteristics of High Reliability
    Organizations," *Organization Science 1* (1990): 160–177.
27. Karlene H. Roberts, Susanne K. Stout, and Jennifer J. Halpern,
    "Decision Dynamics in Two High Reliability Military Organi-
    zations," *Management Science 40* (1994): 622.
28. This possibility is discussed in Paul Keller et al., *Managing the
    Unexpected in Prescribed Fire and Fire Use Operations*, Document
    no. RMRS-GTR-137 (Fort Collins, Colo.: U.S. Department of
    Agriculture, Forest Service, Rocky Mountain Research Station,
    2004), pp. 41–42.
29. National Park Service, *Cerro Grande, Final Report*, p. 45.

30. The expression "high reliability organization" was coined by
    Berkeley researchers Karlene Roberts, Gene Rochlin, and
    Todd LaPorte to capture observed commonalities of opera-
    tions among the carrier *Carl Vinson;* Federal Aviation Admin-
    istration en route air traffic control in Fremont, California;
    and the Diablo Canyon nuclear power generation plant at
    San Luis Obispo, California. In settings such as these, HROs
    operate in an unforgiving environment rich with the potential
    for error, where the scale of consequences precludes learning
    through experimentation and where complex processes are
    used to manage complex technology in order to avoid failures.
    To perform effectively under these conditions, people in
    HROs pursue safety as a priority objective, build in redun-
    dancy, decentralize decision making, shape culture toward re-
    liable performance, invest heavily in training and simulation,
    learn from close calls, aggressively seek to know what they do
    not know, emphasize communication of the big picture and
    where people fit into it, and reward people who report failures;
    see Scott Douglas Sagan, *The Limits of Safety: Organizations,
    Accidents, and Nuclear Weapons* (Princeton, N.J.: Princeton
    University Press, 1993; Karlene H. Roberts and Robert Bea,
    "Must Accidents Happen? Lessons from High-Reliability
    Organizations," *Academy of Management Executive 15* (2001):
    70–78; and Alan Jarman, "'Reliability' Reconsidered: A Cri-
    tique of the HRO-NAT Debate," *Journal of Contingencies and
    Crisis Management 9* (2001): 98–107. The growing literature
    on high reliability is represented by sources such as the follow-
    ing, arranged historically: Gene I. Rochlin, Todd R. LaPorte,
    and Karlene H. Roberts, "The Self-Designing High Reliability
    Organization: Aircraft Carrier Flight Operation at Sea," *Naval
    War College Review 40* (1987): 76–90; Karl E. Weick, "Organi-
    zational Culture as a Source of High Reliability," *California
    Management Review 29* (1987): 112–127; Karlene H. Roberts
    and Denise M. Rousseau, "Research in Nearly Failure-Free,
    High-Reliability Organizations Having the Bubble," *IEEE*

Transactions on Engineering Management 36 (1989): 132–139;
Karlene H. Roberts, "Some Characteristics of High Reliability
Organizations," *Organization Science 1* (1990): 160–177; Paul
R. Schulman, "The Negotiated Order of Organizational Reli-
ability," *Administration and Society 25* (1993): 353–372; Karl E.
Weick and Karlene H. Roberts, "Collective Mind in Organi-
zations: Heedful Interrelating on Flight Decks," *Administrative
Science Quarterly 38* (1993): 357–381; Karlene H. Roberts,
Susanne K. Stout, and Jennifer J. Halpern, "Decision Dynam-
ics in Two High Reliability Military Organizations," *Manage-
ment Science 40* (1994): 614–624; Karl E. Weick, "South
Canyon Revisited: Lessons from High Reliability Organiza-
tions," *Wildfire 4* (1995): 54–68; Todd R. LaPorte, "High
Reliability Organizations: Unlikely, Demanding and at Risk,"
Journal of Contingencies and Crisis Management 4 (1996): 60–71;
Karl E. Weick, Kathleen M. Sutcliffe, and David Obstfeld,
"Organizing for High Reliability: Processes of Collective
Mindfulness," in *Research in Organizational Behavior*, Vol. 21,
ed. Barry M. Staw and Robert I. Sutton (Greenwich, Conn.:
JAI, 1999), pp. 81–123; Karlene H. Roberts and Robert Bea,
"Must Accidents Happen? Lessons from High-Reliability
Organizations," *Academy of Management Executive 15* (2001):
70–78; Paul R. Schulman, "General Attributes of Safe Orga-
nizations," *Quality and Safety in Health Care 13*, Suppl. II
(2004): ii39–ii44; Mathilde Bourrier, "An Interview with
Karlene Roberts," *European Management Journal 23* (2005):
93–97; C. F. Larry Heimann, "Repeated Failures in the Man-
agement of High Risk Technologies," *European Management
Journal 23* (2005): 105–117; Emery Roe, Paul R. Schulman,
Michel van Eeten, and Mark de Bruijne, "High-Reliability
Bandwidth Management in Large Technical Systems: Find-
ings and Implications of Two Case Studies," *Journal of Public
Administration Research and Theory 15* (2005): 263–280; David
L. Cooke and Thomas R. Rohleder, "Learning from Incidents:
From Normal Accidents to High Reliability," *System Dynamics*

Review 22 (2006): 213–239; Peter Madsen, Vinit Desai, Karlene H. Roberts, and Daniel Wong, "Mitigating Hazards Through Continuing Design: The Birth and Evolution of a Pediatric Intensive Care Unit," *Organization Science 17* (2006): 239–248; Emilie M. Roth, Jordan Multer, and Thomas Raslear, "Shared Situation Awareness as a Contributor to High Reliability Performance in Railroad Operations," *Organization Studies 27* (2006): 967–987; and Michal Tamuz and Michael I. Harrison, "Improving Patient Safety in Hospitals: Contributions of High-Reliability Theory and Normal Accident Theory," *Health Services Research 41* (2006): 1654–1676. Criticisms of the literature on high reliability are found in discussions such as Scott Douglas Sagan, *The Limits of Safety: Organizations, Accidents, and Nuclear Weapons* (Princeton, N.J.: Princeton University Press, 1993); Scott Douglas Sagan, "Toward a Political Theory of Organizational Reliability," *Journal of Contingencies and Crisis Management 2* (1994): 228–240; Alan Jarman, "'Reliability' Reconsidered: A Critique of the HRO-NAT Debate," *Journal of Contingencies and Crisis Management 9* (2001): 98–107; Jos A. Rijpma, "From Deadlock to Dead End: The Normal Accidents–High Reliability Debate Revisited," *Journal of Contingencies and Crisis Management 11* (2003): 37–45; and J. S. Busby, "Failure to Mobilize in Reliability-Seeking Organizations: Two Cases from the UK Railways," *Journal of Management Studies 43* (2006): 1375–1393.

31. Schulman, "General Attributes," p. ii39.
32. Barry A. Turner and Nick F. Pidgeon, *Man-Made Disasters*, 2nd ed. (Oxford: Butterworth-Heinemann, 1997), pp. 136–140.

Chapter 2: Expectations and Mindfulness

1. Gene I. Rochlin, Todd R. LaPorte, and Karlene H. Roberts, "The Self-Designing High Reliability Organization: Aircraft Carrier Flight Operation at Sea," *Naval War College Review 40* (1987): 76–90.

2. Karl E. Weick and Karlene H. Roberts, "Collective Mind in Organizations: Heedful Interrelating on Flight Decks," *Administrative Science Quarterly* 38 (1993): 357.

3. Our discussion of properties of expectations draws on James M. Olson, Neal J. Roese, and Mark P. Zanna, "Expectancies," in *Social Psychology: Handbook of Basic Principles*, ed. E. Tory Higgins and Arie W. Kruglanski (New York: Guilford Press, 1996).

4. Ibid., p. 220. In this chapter, we treat *expectation* and *expectancy* as synonyms, with a preference for *expectation* unless material that is quoted uses *expectancy*, as in this case.

5. Lee Clarke, "The Disqualification Heuristic: When Do Organizations Misperceive Risk?" *Research in Social Problems and Public Policy* 5 (1993): 289–312. The basic idea is that people disqualify disconfirming information, highlight confirming information, and neglect information that contradicts a conviction, all in the interest of reducing uncertainty and increasing their sense of control.

6. This is sometimes referred to as the "positive-test strategy" and is discussed in Ziva Kunda, *Social Cognition: Making Sense of People* (Cambridge, Mass.: MIT Press, 1999), pp. 112–120.

7. Mark Snyder and Arthur A. Stukas Jr., "Interpersonal Processes: The Interplay of Cognitive, Motivational, and Behavioral Activities in Social Interaction," *Annual Review of Psychology* 50 (1999): 273–303.

8. Karl E. Weick, "Leadership as the Legitimation of Doubt," in *The Future of Leadership: Today's Top Thinkers on Leadership Speak to the Next Generation*, ed. Warren Bennis, Gretchen M. Spreitzer, and Thomas Cummings (San Francisco: Jossey-Bass, 2001), pp. 91–102.

9. George L. Shackle, *Expectations in Economics* (London: Hyperion, 1979), p. 26.

10. *The 9/11 Commission Report: Final Report of the National Commission on Terrorist Attacks upon the United States* (New York: Norton, 2004), p. 344.

11. See Diane Vaughan, *The Challenger Launch Decision: Risky Technology, Culture, and Deviance at NASA* (Chicago: University of Chicago Press, 1996), pp. 124, 141, 143, and 179.

12. Ibid., p. 249.

13. Eliot A. Cohen and John Gooch, *Military Misfortunes: The Anatomy of Failure in War* (New York: Vintage Books, 1990), p. 44.

14. Mica R. Endsley, "Toward a Theory of Situation Awareness in Dynamic Systems," *Human Factors 37* (1995): 32–64.

15. See Ellen J. Langer, "Minding Matters: The Consequences of Mindlessness-Mindfulness," in *Advances in Experimental Social Psychology*, Vol. 22, ed. Leonard Berkowitz (San Diego, Calif.: Academic Press, 1989), pp. 137–173.

16. Paul R. Schulman, "General Attributes of Safe Organizations," *Quality and Safety in Health Care 13*, Suppl. II (2004): ii39–ii44.

17. See William H. Starbuck and Moshe Farjoun, eds., *Organization at the Limit: Lesson from the Columbia Disaster* (Malden, Mass.: Blackwell, 2005), p. 146.

18. Harold W. Gehman Jr., *Columbia Accident Investigation Board: Report, Volume One* (Washington, D.C.: U.S. Government Printing Office, 2003), p. 122.

19. Bhikkhu Bodhi, *A Comprehensive Manual of Abhidhamma* (Seattle, Wash.: Buddhist Publication Society, Pariyatti Editions, 2000), p. 86.

20. Constance Perin, *Shouldering Risks: The Culture of Control in the Nuclear Power Industry* (Princeton, N.J.: Princeton University Press, 2006), p. 267.

21. Gene I. Rochlin, "Informal Organizational Networking as a Crisis-Avoidance Strategy: U.S. Naval Flight Operations as a Case Study," *Organization and Environment 3* (1989): 159–176.

22. See Linda T. Kohn, Janet M. Corrigan, and Molla S. Donaldson, eds., *To Err Is Human: Building a Safer Health System* (Washington, D.C.: National Academy Press, 1999), pp. 160–162.

23. James T. Reason, *Managing the Risks of Organizational Accidents* (Brookfield, Vt.: Ashgate, 1997), p. 37. The background for

this depiction is found in Karl E. Weick, "Organizational Culture as a Source of High Reliability," *California Management Review 2* (1987): 112–127.

Chapter 3: The Three Principles of Anticipation

1. Our understanding of nuclear power plants has been advanced significantly by the work of Constance Perin, *Shouldering Risks: The Culture of Control in the Nuclear Power Industry* (Princeton, N.J.: Princeton University Press, 2006); Paul R. Schulman, "The Analysis of High Reliability Organizations: A Comparative Framework," in *New Challenges to Understanding Organizations*, ed. Karlene H. Roberts (Old Tappan, N.J.: Macmillan, 1993), pp. 33–54; Paul R. Schulman, "General Attributes of Safe Organizations," *Quality and Safety in Health Care 13*, Suppl. II (2004): ii39–ii44; and Paul R. Schulman, "The Negotiated Order of Organizational Reliability," *Administration and Society 25* (1993): 353–372. Their influence is abundantly clear in the frequent citations to their work in Chapters Three and Four.

2. Schulman, "Negotiated Order," pp. 357–358. Nuclear power plant operations require almost four times as many employees as conventional fossil-fueled steam-generating plants to produce a similar amount of electricity and operate reliably. At the Diablo Canyon nuclear power plant in San Luis Obispo, California, for example, there are approximately 1,250 employees on site during standard operations. During scheduled maintenance overhauls or outages, this number increases dramatically with the addition of over 1,100 outside consultants, support staff, and service contract workers. In contrast, a conventional fossil-fueled steam-generating plant located near Pittsburg, California, has 287 employees on site and typically needs no more than 25 additional employees under contract to do its largest overhaul job.

3. Perin, *Shouldering Risks*, p. 263.

4. Ibid., pp. 203–204.

5. Ibid., p. 19.

6. Ibid., p. 134.

7. Ibid., p. xv.

8. Ibid., p. 265.

9. *MMWR Recommended Reports*, 47 RR-15, Sept. 11, 1998, p. 7.

10. This is the concept of abduction and is discussed by Perin, *Shouldering Risks*, p. 215, and by Gerardo Patriotta, *Organizational Knowledge in the Making: How Firms Create, Use and Institutionalize Knowledge* (Oxford: Oxford University Press, 2004).

11. Henry Mintzberg, *The Rise and Fall of Strategic Planning* (New York: Free Press, 1994), ch. 5.

12. A Google search on this phrase returns over half a million entries, one of which indicates that the phrase is trademarked by Alan M. Blankstein.

13. Perin, *Shouldering Risks*, p. 216.

14. Ibid., p. ix.

15. Ibid.

16. Ibid., p. 185.

17. Ibid., pp. 49–55.

18. See James T. Reason, *Managing the Risks of Organizational Accidents* (Brookfield, Vt.: Ashgate, 1997), p. 91.

19. For a detailed answer to this question, see U.S. Nuclear Regulatory Commission (NRC), *Davis-Besse Reactor Vessel, Head Degradation Lessons-Learned Task Force Report* (Washington, D.C.: U.S. Nuclear Regulatory Commission, September 30, 2002). The NRC's senior management review and commentary on the lessons-learned report is found in Carl J. Paperiello, *Senior Management Review of the Lessons-Learned Report for the Degradation of the Davis-Besse Nuclear Power Station Reactor Pressure Vessel Head* (Washington, D.C.: U.S. Nuclear Regulatory Commission, November 28, 2002).

20. Perin, *Shouldering Risks*, p. 272.

21. Ron Westrum, "Cultures with Requisite Imagination," in *Verification and Validation of Complex Systems: Human Factors Issues*, ed. John A. Wise, V. David Hopkin, and Paul Stager (New York: Springer-Verlag, 1993), pp. 401–416.

22. Martin Landau and Donald Chisholm, "The Arrogance of Optimism: Notes on Failure Avoidance Management," *Journal of Contingencies and Crisis Management 3* (1995): 67–80.

23. Amy C. Edmondson, "Psychological Safety and Learning Behavior in Work Teams," *Administrative Science Quarterly 44* (1999): 350–383.

24. For a contrasting view and references supporting it, see Timothy J. Vogus and Kathleen M. Sutcliffe, "The Safety Organizing Scale: Development and Validation of a Behavioral Measure of Safety Culture in Hospital Nursing Units," *Medical Care 45* (2007): 46–54; and Timothy J. Vogus and Kathleen M. Sutcliffe, "The Impact of Safety Organizing, Supportive Leadership, and Care Pathways on Reported Medication Errors in Hospital Nursing Units," *Medical Care*, in press.

25. See John S. Carroll, "Organizational Learning Activities in High-Hazard Industries: The Logics Underlying Self-Analysis," *Journal of Management Studies 35* (1998): 699–717.

26. James T. Reason, "Human Error: Models and Management," *British Medical Journal 320* (2000): 768–770. The following description of the Swiss cheese model is from "Anatomy of an Error," posted on the "Patient Safety–Quality Improvement" page of the Duke University Medical Center's Web site, http://patientsafetyed.duhs.duke.edu/module_e/swiss_cheese.html, accessed on Mar. 30, 2007:

Every step in a process has the potential for failure, to varying degrees. "The ideal system is analogous to a stack of slices of Swiss cheese. Consider the holes to be opportunities for a process to fail, and each of the slices as "defensive layers" in the process. An error may allow a problem to pass through a hole in one layer, but in the next layer the holes are in different places, and the problem should be caught. Each layer is a *defense* against potential error impacting the outcome.

For a catastrophic error to occur, the holes need to align for each step in the process allowing all defenses to be defeated and resulting in an error. If the layers are set up with all the holes lined up, this is an inherently flawed system that will allow a problem at the beginning to progress all the way through to adversely affect the outcome. Each slice of cheese is an opportunity to stop an error. The more defenses you put up, the better. Also the fewer the holes and the smaller the holes, the more likely you are to catch/stop errors that may occur.

27. William H. Starbuck and Frances J. Milliken, "Challenger: Fine-Tuning the Odds Until Something Breaks," *Journal of Management Studies* 25 (1988): 329–330. A number of other scholars have documented the liabilities of success. See, for example, Danny Miller, "The Architecture of Simplicity," *Academy of Management Review* 18 (1993): 116–138; and Sim B. Sitkin, "Learning Through Failure: The Strategy of Small Losses," in *Research in Organizational Behavior*, Vol. 14, ed. Barry M. Staw and Larry L. Cummings (Greenwich, Conn.: JAI Press), pp. 231–266.
28. Haridimos Tsoukas, *Complex Knowledge: Studies in Organizational Epistemology* (Oxford: Oxford University Press, 2005), p. 124.
29. Harold W. Gehman Jr., *Columbia Accident Investigation Board Report*, Vol. 1 (Washington, D.C.: U.S. Government Printing Office, 2003), p. 122.
30. Perin, *Shouldering Risks*, p. 219.
31. Ibid., pp. 219–222.
32. Schulman, "Analysis of High Reliability Organizations," p. 43.
33. Ibid., p. 47.
34. See J. Stuart Bunderson and Kathleen M. Sutcliffe, "Comparing Alternative Conceptualizations of Functional Diversity in Management Teams: Process and Performance Effects," *Academy of Management Journal* 45 (2003): 875–893; and J. Stuart

Bunderson and Kathleen M. Sutcliffe, "When to Put the Brakes on Learning," *Harvard Business Review*, February 2003, pp. 20–21.

35. Schulman, "Analysis of High Reliability Organizations," p. 44.

36. Reuben M. Baron and Stephen J. Misovich, "On the Relationship Between Social and Cognitive Modes of Organization," in *Dual-Process Theories in Social Psychology*, ed. Shelly Chaiken and Yaacov Trope (New York: Guilford Press, 1999), pp. 586–605.

37. Patriotta, *Organizational Knowledge in the Making*.

38. See Perin, *Shouldering Risks*, p. 219.

39. John A. Meacham, "The Loss of Wisdom," in *Wisdom*, ed. Robert J. Sternberg (New York: Cambridge University Press, 1990), pp. 181–211.

40. Karlene H. Roberts, "Structuring to Facilitate Migrating Decisions in Reliability Enhancing Organizations," in *Advances in Global High-Technology Management*, Vol. 2, ed. Luis R. Gomez-Mejia and Michael W. Lawless (Greenwich, Conn.: JAI Press, 1992), p. 183.

41. Schulman, "Negotiated Order," p. 364.

42. Mathilde Bourrier, "Organizing Maintenance Work at Two Nuclear Power Plants," *Journal of Contingencies and Crisis Management 21* (1996): 104–112.

43. Perin, *Shouldering Risks*, p. xvi.

44. Ibid., p. 26.

45. Kathleen M. Eisenhardt, "Making Fast Strategic Decisions in High-Velocity Environments," *Academy of Management Journal 32* (1989): 543–576.

46. Perin, *Shouldering Risks*, p. 62.

47. Ibid.

Chapter 4: Principles of Containment

1. Erik E. Hollnagel, *Barriers and Accident Prevention* (Burlington, Vt.: Ashgate, 2004), p. 7.

2. Henry Mintzberg, *The Rise and Fall of Strategic Planning* (New York: Free Press, 1994), ch. 5.

3. Larry Hirschhorn, "Hierarchy Versus Bureaucracy: The Case of a Nuclear Reactor," in *New Challenges to Understanding Organizations*, ed. Karlene H. Roberts (Old Tappan, N.J.: Macmillan, 1993), p. 139.

4. Paul R. Schulman, "The Negotiated Order of Organizational Reliability," *Administration and Society* 25 (1993): 353–372.

5. James T. Reason, *Managing the Risks of Organizational Accidents* (Brookfield, Vt.: Ashgate, 1997), p. 25.

6. Stephen S. Morse, *Emerging Viruses* (New York: Oxford University Press, 1993); Clarence J. Peters, *Virus Hunter: Thirty Years of Battling Hot Viruses Around the World* (New York: Anchor/Doubleday, 1997); Frank Ryan, *Virus X: Tracking the New Killer Plagues* (New York: Little Brown, 1997).

7. Robin Marantz Henig, *A Dancing Matrix: How Science Confronts Emerging Viruses* (New York: Vintage Books, 1993), p. 193.

8. Ibid., pp. 193–194.

9. Aaron Wildavsky, *Searching for Safety* (New Brunswick, N.J.: Transaction, 1991), p. 120.

10. Ibid., p. 221.

11. Brad Allenby and Jonathan Fink, "Toward Inherently Secure and Resilient Societies," *Science*, August 12, 2005, p. 1034.

12. John Wreathall, "Properties of Resilient Organizations: An Initial View," in *Resilience Engineering: Concepts and Precepts*, ed. Erik Hollnagel, David D. Woods, and Nancy Leveson (Burlington, Vt.: Ashgate, 2006), p. 276.

13. George A. Bonanno, "Loss, Trauma, and Human Resilience: How We Underestimated the Human Capacity to Strive After Extremely Aversive Events," *American Psychologist* 59 (2004): 20–28.

14. Erik Hollnagel and David D. Woods, "Epilogue: Resilience Engineering Precepts," in *Resilience Engineering: Concepts and Precepts*, ed. Erik Hollnagel, David D. Woods, and Nancy Leveson (Burlington, Vt.: Ashgate, 2006), p. 348.

15. We are indebted to Amy Wrzesniewski for her efforts on Mar. 23, 2006, to track down this information.

16. Reason, *Managing the Risks*, p. 49.

17. Kathleen M. Sutcliffe and Timothy J. Vogus, "Organizing for Resilience," in *Positive Organizational Scholarship*, ed. Kim S. Cameron, Jane E. Dutton, and Robert E. Quinn (San Francisco: Berrett-Koehler, 2003), pp. 94–110.

18. Schulman, "Negotiated Order," pp. 364–365.

19. Ibid., p. 362.

20. Karlene H. Roberts, Susanne K. Stout, and Jennifer J. Halpern, "Decision Dynamics in Two High Reliability Military Organizations," *Management Science* 40 (1994): 622.

21. Karl E. Weick, "Making Sense of Blurred Images: Mindful Organizing in Mission STS-107," in *Organization at the Limit: Lessons from the* Columbia *Disaster*, ed. William H. Starbuck and Moshe Farjoun (Malden, Mass.: Blackwell, 2005), pp. 159–178.

22. Harold W. Gehman Jr., *Columbia Accident Investigation Board Report*, Vol. 1 (Washington, D.C.: U.S. Government Printing Office, 2003), p. 172.

23. Ibid., p. 154.

24. Ibid., p. 158.

25. Ibid., p. 200.

26. Ibid., p. 149.

27. Ibid., p. 149.

28. Ibid., p. 119.

29. Ibid., p. 149.

30. Ibid., p. 169.

31. Ibid., p. 201.

32. Andrew Hopkins, *Safety, Culture and Risk: The Organisational Causes of Disasters* (North Ryde, New South Wales: CCH Australia, 2005), p. 13.

33. Constance Perin, *Shouldering Risks: The Culture of Control in the Nuclear Power Industry* (Princeton, N.J.: Princeton University Press, 2006), p. 93.

34. Ibid., p. 257.
35. Karlene H. Roberts, "Structuring to Facilitate Migrating Decisions in Reliability Enhancing Organizations," in *Advances in Global High-Technology Management*, Vol. 2, ed. Luis R. Gomez-Mejia and Michael W. Lawless (Greenwich, Conn.: JAI Press, 1992), p. 179.
36. Mathilde Bourrier, "Organizing Maintenance at Two Nuclear Power Plants," *Journal of Contingencies and Crisis Management* 21 (1996): 109.
37. Karl E. Weick, Kathleen M. Sutcliffe, and David Obstfeld, "Organizing for High Reliability: Processes of Collective Mindfulness, in *Research in Organizational Behavior*, Vol. 21, ed. Barry M. Staw and Robert I. Sutton (Greenwich, Conn.: JAI Press, 1999), p. 102.
38. See Karl E. Weick and Karlene H. Roberts, "Collective Mind in Organizations: Heedful Interrelating on Flight Decks," *Administrative Science Quarterly* 38 (1993): 357–381.
39. Gene I. Rochlin, "Informal Organizational Networking as a Crisis-Avoidance Strategy: U.S. Naval Flight Operations as a Case Study," *Industrial Crisis Quarterly* 3 (1989): 167.
40. Schulman, "Negotiated Order," p. 365.
41. Perin, *Shouldering Risks*, p. 79.
42. Gehman, *Columbia Accident Investigation Board Report*, p. 201.

Chapter 5: Assessing Your Capabilities for Resilient Performance

1. Robert E. Allinson, *Global Disasters: Inquiries into Management Ethics* (Upper Saddle River, N.J.: Prentice Hall, 1993), p. 11.
2. Ibid., p. 193.
3. Ibid.
4. Paul R. Schulman, "General Attributes of Safe Organizations," *Quality and Safety in Health Care 13*, Suppl. II (2004): ii39.
5. Ellen J. Langer, "Minding Matters: The Consequences of Mindlessness-Mindfulness," in *Advances in Experimental Social*

Psychology, Vol. 22, ed. Leonard Berkowitz (San Diego: Academic Press, 1989), pp. 137–173.

6. Ron Westrum, "Organizational and Interorganizational Thought," paper presented at the World Bank Conference on Safety Control and Risk Management, 1988.

7. See James T. Reason, *Managing the Risks of Organizational Accidents* (Brookfield, Vt.: Ashgate, 1997), p. 91.

8. Charles Perrow, *Normal Accidents: Living with High-Risk Technologies* (New York: Basic Books, 1984).

9. See Scott Douglas Sagan, *The Limits of Safety: Organizations, Accidents, and Nuclear Weapons* (Princeton, N.J.: Princeton University Press, 1993), p. 34.

10. Ibid., p. 33.

11. Timothy J. Vogus, "In Search of Mechanisms: How Do HR Practices Affect Organizational Performance?" doctoral dissertation, University of Michigan, 2004.

12. A validation analysis of the MOS can be found in Timothy J. Vogus and Kathleen M. Sutcliffe, "The Safety Organizing Scale: Development and Validation of a Behavioral Measure of Safety Culture in Hospital Nursing Units," *Medical Care 45* (2007): 46–54. Validation refers to the extent to which a measure purportedly measures what it is supposed to measure. Vogus and Sutcliffe found that the nine-item measure of self-reported behaviors had high internal reliability and discriminated between related concepts such as organizational commitment and trust. Moreover, high scores on the MOS were associated with lower levels of reported medication errors and patient falls in the period after the original survey was conducted. In a related paper titled "The Impact of Safety Organizing, Supportive Leadership, and Care Pathways on Reported Medication Errors in Hospital Nursing Units," *Medical Care*, in press, Vogus and Sutcliffe reported that a 1-point increase in mindful organizing on a 7-point scale resulted in almost a 30 percent decrease in the expected number of medication errors six months later.

Chapter 6: Organizational Culture: Institutionalizing Mindfulness

1. Barry A. Turner and Nick F. Pidgeon, *Man-Made Disasters*, 2nd ed. (Oxford: Butterworth-Heinemann, 1997), p. 47.
2. Ibid., p. 102.
3. Debra Meyerson and Joanne Martin, "Cultural Change: An Integration of Three Different Views," *Journal of Management Studies 24* (1987): 623–647.
4. Edgar H. Schein, "Culture: The Missing Concept in Organization Studies," *Administrative Science Quarterly 41* (1996): 229–240.
5. W. Ross Ashby, *Introduction to Cybernetics* (New York: Wiley, 1956), ch. 11.
6. Meyerson and Martin, "Cultural Change," p. 637.
7. James T. Reason, *Managing the Risks of Organizational Accidents* (Brookfield, Vt.: Ashgate, 1997), p. 294.
8. Ibid.
9. Karl E. Weick, "Sensemaking in Organizations: Small Structures with Large Consequences," in *Social Psychology in Organizations: Advances in Theory and Research*, ed. J. Keith Murnighan (Upper Saddle River, N.J.: Prentice Hall, 1993), pp. 10–37.
10. Edgar H. Schein, *Organizational Culture and Leadership* (San Francisco: Jossey-Bass, 1985), ch. 1.
11. This close blending of culture with expectations has been noted by other researchers of culture, including Charles A. O'Reilly and Jennifer A. Chatman, "Culture as Social Control: Corporations, Cults, and Commitment," in *Research in Organizational Behavior*, Vol. 18, ed. by Barry M. Staw and Larry L. Cummings (Greenwich, Conn.: JAI Press, 1996), p. 160, who describe culture as a social control system based on shared norms and values that set expectations about appropriate attitudes and behavior for members of the group. See also Jennifer A. Chatman and Sandra Eunyoung Cha, "Lead-

ing by Leveraging Culture," *California Management Review* 45 (Summer 2003): 20–34; Edgar H. Schein, *The Corporate Culture Survival Guide: Sense and Nonsense About Culture Change* (San Francisco: Jossey-Bass, 1999); and Mary Jo Hatch, "The Dynamics of Organizational Culture," *Academy of Management Review* 18 (1993): 657–693. Hatch, who has made important extensions of Schein's ideas, has paid close attention to the ways in which assumptions are manifested in values and the ways in which values are realized in artifacts. She notes:

Assumptions provide expectations that influence perceptions, thoughts, and feelings about the world and the organization. These perceptions, thoughts, and feelings are then experienced as reflecting the world and the organization. Members recognize among these reflections aspects they both like and dislike, and on this basis they become conscious of their values (without necessarily being conscious of the basic assumptions on which their experiences and values are based). . . . Realization follows manifestation only if expectations and their associated values find their way into activity that has tangible outcomes. Many different activities can contribute to the realization of expectations: among them are the production of objects (e.g., company products, official reports, internal newsletters, buildings); engagement in organizational events (e.g., meetings, company picnics, award banquets, office parties); [and] participation in discourse (e.g., formal speeches, informal conversation, joking) [pp. 662, 666].

12. Thomas J. Peters and Robert H. Waterman Jr., *In Search of Excellence: Lessons from America's Best-Run Companies* (New York: HarperCollins, 1982), p. 322.
13. Charles O'Reilly, "Corporations, Culture, and Commitment: Motivation and Social Control in Organizations," *California Management Review* 31 (1989): 9–25.
14. CBS News, *48 Hours*, "Supercarrier," July 26, 1990.
15. Andrew Hopkins, *Safety, Culture and Risk: The Organisational Causes of Disasters* (North Ryde, New South Wales: CCH Australia, 2005), p. 7.

16. Richard I Cook, personal communication, Jan. 29, 2004.
17. Schein, *Corporate Culture Survival Guide*, p. 189.
18. Why $65? It cost Continental $5 million a month for being late (in payments for housing and meals for those who missed connections, payments to other airlines, and crew overtime, among other things). If you're on time, you save $5 million. Take half of that sum and give it back to the employees ($2.5 million divided by 40,000 people equals $65 per month). See Gordon Bethune, *From Worst to First* (New York: Wiley, 1998), pp. 102–103.
19. Ibid., p. 138.
20. Gerald R. Salancik, "Commitment and the Control of Organizational Behavior and Belief," in *New Directions in Organizational Behavior*, ed. Barry M. Staw and Gerald R. Salancik (Chicago: St. Clair Press, 1977), pp. 1–54.
21. This scenario is based on an actual incident involving a different firm reported in Michael L. Tushman and Charles A. O'Reilly III, *Winning Through Innovation: A Practical Guide to Leading Organizational Change and Renewal* (Boston: Harvard Business School Press, 1997).
22. James T. Reason, "Human Error: Models and Management," *British Medical Journal 320* (2000): 770.
23. James T. Reason, "Achieving a Safe Culture: Theory and Practice," *Work and Stress 12* (1998): 294.
24. *The Report of the Public Inquiry into Children's Heart Surgery at the Bristol Royal Infirmary, 1984–1995: Learning from Bristol*, Document no. CM 5207 (London: Stationery Office, July 2001), p. 241, para. 21. (Each paragraph in each chapter of this report is numbered.)
25. Ibid., p. 248, para. 6; emphasis added.
26. Ibid., p. 23.
27. Ibid., p. 25.
28. Ibid., p. 104.
29. These data are available at http://www.Bristol-inquiry.org.uk.
30. Julian Savulescu, "Beyond Bristol: Taking Responsibility," *Journal of Medical Ethics 28* (2002): 281–282.

31. *Report of the Public Inquiry:* a provider-oriented culture (p. 257); a culture of blame (p. 16); a club culture where one's career depends on whether one fit into the inner circle (p. 302) and not on one's performance (p. 68); a culture of fear (p. 201); an oral culture (p. 202); a culture of justification (p. 161); a culture of paternalism (p. 268); a culture of uncertainty (p. 273).

32. Ibid., p. 163.

33. Ibid., p. 202, para. 17.

34. Ibid., p. 269, para. 19.

35. Ibid., p. 177.

36. Ibid., p. 210, para. 13.

37. Ibid., p. 200, para. 14.

38. Ibid., p. 240, para. 17.

39. For example, patients are given unduly optimistic information to gain their compliance (ibid., p. 288), and mortality data are collected by regional authorities but are not analyzed because regional personnel describe themselves as fundraisers, not monitors of quality of care (p. 188, para 7).

40. Ibid., p. 16, para. 84.

41. Reason, *Managing the Risks*, p. 195.

42. Reason, "Achieving a Safe Culture," p. 303.

43. Reason, *Managing the Risks*, p. 11.

44. *Report of the Public Inquiry*, p. 77, para. 4.

45. Ibid., p. 259, para. 19.

46. Ibid., para. 20.

47. Diane Vaughan, *The Challenger Launch Decision: Risky Technology, Culture, and Deviance at NASA* (Chicago: University of Chicago Press, 1996), pp. 392–393.

48. *Report of the Public Inquiry*, p. 243, para. 24; emphasis added.

49. Ibid., p. 267, para. 12.

50. Ibid., p. 215, para. 34.

51. Ibid., p. 209.

52. An especially insightful discussion of organizational learning mechanisms is found in Raanan Lipshitz, Victor J. Friedman, and Micha Popper, *Demystifying Organizational Learning* (Thousand Oaks, Calif.: Sage, 2007).

53. *Report of the Public Inquiry*, p. 248, para. 4.

54. Ibid., p. 272, para. 27.

55. Ibid., p. 300, para. 55.

56. Ibid., p. 297, para. 50.

57. Ibid., p. 248, para. 4.

58. Ibid., p. 143, para. 55.

59. Ibid., p. 144, para. 59.

60. Ibid., pp. 364–365, para. 28.

Chapter 7: How to Manage Mindfully

1. Dave R. Schwandt, "When Managers Become Philosophers: Integrating Learning with Sensemaking," *Academy of Management Learning and Education* 4 (2005): 176–192.

2. Karl E. Weick, "Small Wins: Redefining the Scale of Social Problems," *American Psychologist* 39 (1984): 43.

3. National Interagency Fire Center, "Wildland Fire Statistics: Prescribed Fires and Acres by Agency," http://www.nifc.gov/stats/prescribed_fires.html, accessed Mar. 30, 2007.

4. The Ten Standard Firefighting Orders: (1) Keep informed on fire weather conditions and forecasts. (2) Know what your fire is doing at all times. (3) Base all actions on current and expected behavior of the fire. (4) Identify escape routes and safety zones and make them known. (5) Post lookouts when there is possible danger. (6) Be alert. Keep calm. Think clearly. Act decisively. (7) Maintain prompt communications with your forces, your supervisor, and adjoining forces. (8) Give clear instructions and ensure they are understood. (9) Maintain control of your forces at all times. (10) Fight fire aggressively, having provided for safety first.

5. Ted Putnam, *The Ten Standard Firefighting Orders: Can Anyone Follow Them?* (Missoula, Mont.: Mindful Solutions, 2001).

6. Karl Brauneis, "'Original Intent': Ten Standard Firefighting Orders," *Smokejumper Magazine* (2001), http://www.wildland fire.com/docs/2003_n_before/10fireorders.htm, accessed Mar.

30, 2007: (1) Know what your FIRE is doing at all times. (2) Base all actions on current and expected BEHAVIOR of the FIRE. (3) Keep informed on FIRE WEATHER conditions and forecasts. (4) Post a LOOKOUT when there is possible danger. (5) Have ESCAPE ROUTES for everyone and make sure they are known (safety zones). (6) Be ALERT, keep CALM, THINK clearly, and ACT decisively. (7) Maintain CONTROL of your men at all times. (8) Give clear INSTRUCTIONS and be sure they are understood. (9) Maintain prompt COMMUNICATION with your men, your boss, and adjoining forces. (10) Fight fire aggressively but provide for SAFETY first.

7. See National Interagency Fire Center, "Safety," http://www.nifc.gov/safety_study/10-18-lces.html, accessed May 7, 2007.

8. Paula Nasiatka, "Line Officer Lessons Learned," *Scratchline* (newsletter of the Wildland Fire Lessons Learned Center), Nov. 2006; interview with Darlene M. Koontz, superintendent of Bandelier National Monument http://www.wildfirelessons. net/documents/Scratchline_Issue18.pdf, accessed Mar. 30, 2007.

9. Paul Keller and Brett Fay, eds., *Hawkins Wildland Fire Use Staff Ride Preliminary Study: Staff Ride Information and Advance Study Packet for the Hawkins Fire Use Staff Ride, Dixie National Forest*, May 24–25, 2005. The Region 4 Fire and Aviation Management Program requested and funded the report.

10. Wildland Fire Leadership Development Program, "About Staff Rides," http://www.fireleadership.gov/toolbox/staffride/main_about_staff_rides.html, accessed Mar. 30, 2007.

11. For survey data suggesting that AARs generate mixed reactions, see Curt Braun, "After Action Review Survey: Findings and Recommendations: Wedge Canyon and Robert Fires Glacier National Park Montana, 2003," report submitted to the Wildland Fire Lessons Learned Center, Aug. 2004.

12. Wildland Fire Lessons Learned Center, "New Mission Statement," http://www.wildfirelessons.net, accessed May 7, 2007.

13. Procedures used in a peer review have now been expanded and made more formal in a procedure called "Facilitated

Learning Analysis." Still, a peer review process is described as follows (Little Venus Fire Shelter Deployment, July 24, 2006, pp. 34–35):

Peer Review Panel Composition. . . . The process centers around convening a small panel of respected operators, known for their ability to perform the particular mission in the particular environment, and also known to be insightful, fair, just, and honest. It is imperative that the panel and its members be able to create an open "listening" environment. Peer Review Panels are an opportunity to involve future leaders to help them expand their understanding of the diversity and complexity of fire operations, and broaden their vision of the fire program they will eventually inherit. Questions . . . are designed to ascertain each interviewee's perspective. The panel will combine a number of these perspectives to develop a picture of the event, internal and external influences, and the decisions and behaviors involved. . . . The panel should continue questioning in areas where the reviewers feel disconnect, discomfort, confusion, or curiosity. . . . It is important to understand that Peer Review Panel activities are entirely focused on developing lessons learned, and not to contribute to other investigations or reviews.

14. Loren Snell, Randy Smith, Rod Dykehouse, Elden Alexander, and Steve Holdsambeck, "Peer Review Report of Balls Canyon Near-Miss, June 27th, 2006, Humboldt-Toiyabe National Forest," http://www.wildfirelessons.net/documents/Balls_Canyon_Near_Miss_062706_Final_Report.pdf, accessed Mar. 30, 2007, p. 18.
15. TriData Corporation, *Wildland Firefighter Safety Awareness Study: Phase III—Implementing Cultural Changes for Safety* (March 1998), pp. v–vi.
16. Ibid., "Executive Summary," italics in the original.
17. Edgar H. Schein, *The Corporate Culture Survival Guide* (San Francisco: Jossey-Bass, 1999), pp. 124–126.
18. Suzy Wetlaufer, "Organizing for Empowerment: An Interview with AES's Roger Sant and Dennis Bakke," *Harvard Business Review*, Jan.-Feb. 1999, p. 114.

19. V. De Keyser and David D. Woods, "Fixation Errors: Failures to Revise Situation Assessment in Dynamic and Risky Systems," in *Systems Reliability Assessment*, ed. A. G. Colombo and Amalio Saiz de Bustamante (Dordrecht, Netherlands: Kluwer Academic, 1990). See also Jenny Rudolph, "Adaptive Sensemaking: Combining Exploration and Exploitation in Operating Room Crises," working paper, Boston University School of Public Health, 2007.

20. See Gary Klein, Rebecca Pliske, Beth Crandall, and David D. Woods, "Problem Detection," *Cognition, Technology and Work* 7 (2005): 14–28.

21. See Gary Klein, *Sources of Power: How People Make Decisions* (Cambridge, Mass.: MIT Press, 1998), p. 274.

22. For a discussion of media richness, see Richard L. Daft and Robert H. Lengel, "Information Richness: A New Approach to Manager Information Processing and Organization Design," *in Research in Organizational Behavior*, Vol. 6, ed. Barry M. Staw and Larry L. Cummings (Greenwich, Conn.: JAI Press, 1984), pp. 191–233.

23. Gary Klein, *Intuition at Work* (New York: Doubleday, 2003).

24. Ron Westrum, "Cultures with Requisite Imagination," in *Verification and Validation of Complex Systems: Human Factors Issues*, ed. John A. Wise, V. David Hopkin, and Paul Stager (New York: Springer-Verlag, 1993), pp. 401–416; Ron Westrum, "Management Strategies and Information Failure," in *Information Systems: Failure Analysis*, ed. John A. Wise and Anthony Debons (New York: Springer-Verlag, 1987), pp. 109–127; Ron Westrum, "Thinking by Groups, Organizations, and Networks: A Sociologist's View of the Social Psychology of Science and Technology," in *The Social Psychology of Science*, ed. William R. Shadish and Steve Fuller (New York: Guilford Press, 1993), pp. 329–342.

The Authors

Karl E. Weick is the Rensis Likert Distinguished University Professor of Organizational Behavior and Psychology at the University of Michigan. He joined the Stephen M. Ross School of Business at the University of Michigan in 1988 after previous faculty positions at the University of Texas, Cornell University, the University of Minnesota, and Purdue University. He received his Ph.D. from Ohio State University in social and organizational psychology. He is a former editor of the journal *Administrative Science Quarterly* (1977–1985) and former associate editor of the journal *Organizational Behavior and Human Performance* (1971–1977).

Weick's book *The Social Psychology of Organizing*, first published in 1969 and revised in 1979, was designated one of the nine best business books ever written by *Inc.* magazine in December 1996. This work has also been profiled in *Wired* magazine and by Peters and Waterman in their book *In Search of Excellence*. The organizing formulation has more recently been expanded into a book titled *Sensemaking in Organizations* (Sage, 1995). Weick was presented with the Irwin Award for Distinguished Scholarly Contributions by the Academy of Management in 1990. In the same year, he received the Best Article of the Year award from the *Academy of Management Review* for his article "Theory Construction as Disciplined Imagination."

Weick's research interests include collective sensemaking under pressure, handoffs and transitions in dynamic events, organizing for resilient performance, and continuous change.

Kathleen M. Sutcliffe is the Gilbert and Ruth Whitaker Professor of Business Administration and professor of management and organizations at the Stephen M. Ross School of Business at the University of Michigan. She joined the Ross School in 1994 and before that held a faculty position in the Carlson School of Management at the University of Minnesota. Prior to completing her Ph.D. in management from the University of Texas at Austin in 1991, she lived and worked in Juneau, Alaska, as a program consultant for the state of Alaska and also in Anchorage, Alaska, as a senior manager for the Aleutian Pribilof Islands Association, one of the regional Alaska Native health corporations.

In 2006, Sutcliffe received the Researcher of the Year award from the Stephen M. Ross School of Business for her research excellence. Her research interests include topics such as organizational resilience and reliability, how organizations and their members sense emerging problems and cope with uncertainty, cognitive and experiential diversity in top management teams, and team and organizational learning. Her most recent work examines how elements of an organizational system influence errors in health care settings. Her work has been published in a wide variety of journals, including the *Academy of Management Review*, the *Academy of Management Journal*, *California Management Review*, and the *Harvard Business Review*.

Sutcliffe teaches the fundamentals of leading change in the executive M.B.A. program and the fundamentals of human and organizational behavior in the M.B.A. program.

Index